LEARN FROM FAILURE
THE KEY TO SUCCESSFUL DECISION-MAKING

ROBERT V. SICINA

Kravitz & Sons

Kravitz and Sons LLC
1301 Farmville Blvd, Suite 104
Greenville, NC 27834

Published by Kravitz and Sons LLC.
ISBN: 979-8-89639-269-9 (sc)
ISBN: 979-8-89639-270-5 (e)

Library of Congress Control Number: 2025912723

To all the students of my Learn from Failure course, who have taught me so much about understanding failure, inspired me to work hard to deepen my understanding of failure, and encouraged me to write this book. It is also dedicated to my better half, Colette, without whose understanding and patience with my work ethic this book could have never been written. And finally, it is dedicated to my two sons, Marc and Nick, whose belief in me has been a continual source of renewal and energy.

WARNING: THIS BOOK MAY NOT BE FOR YOU.

Author's note: This book contains stories from true events as best I remember them. For most, the names of those involved have been changed, and details of the circumstances have been altered to protect the identities of all the parties involved.

Please review the following questions:

- When one of your decisions goes bad, do you find it's often not bad luck or somebody else's fault? It's your own.
- Do you believe your track record in decision-making could be a lot better?
- Do you sometimes find yourself confused trying to understand why you failed?

ACKNOWLEDGMENTS

There were many people who helped me along in my journey of writing this book. I won't try to name them all for fear of forgetting some. Rather, I want to acknowledge one person, Colonel Thomas X. Hammes, US Marine Corps (retired), or TX as he's known.

When I was developing the course for the honors program and came up with the hypothesis that the drivers of failure in decision-making were the same in business, international development, and warfare, I thought I knew something about international development. I didn't—but I knew that I knew nothing about warfare. So, I embarked on a search to find someone locally who did. It didn't take long for me to find TX and invite him to lunch. I was surprised when he said yes. TX is an accomplished author. His *The Sling and the Stone* has sold more than fifty thousand copies in spite of having a fairly narrow target of military strategists and historians.

Over lunch, I talked about my hypotheses and showed him the Cube (you will be introduced to the Cube in chapter 1). He immediately said, "Looks to me like you have the makings of a book here." I laughed and said I couldn't imagine myself writing a book. TX said he never thought of himself as writing a book. He always felt he was writing fifteen twenty-page papers. I laughed and explained that I had my undergraduate degree in electrical engineering and I went on to get an MBA in finance. I had never written anything longer than three pages in my life.

So, five years ago, I embarked on the journey—and TX went along with me. He edited every chapter and did so brilliantly. He was even patient with me while I took two and a half years to write chapter 4! Needless to say, without TX, there would be no book. Thanks very much, TX. Semper fi!

PREFACE

About sixteen years ago, I was asked by my employer, the American University Kogod School of Business, to develop a new course. I was given a blank sheet of paper. Amusingly, the senior associate dean, Tom Vonk, candidly admitted late one Friday evening that he had "asked every other faculty member to do it—and they all turned me down." At that point, I had a whopping one year of experience in the classroom. I jumped at the chance because my goal has always been to add value wherever I go. Plus, I loved teaching, but, as an executive in residence, I could never be tenured. This course was a way to demonstrate how I might uniquely contribute.

I slept on it and concluded that one of the most important ways I had learned in my life was through failure both personally (painful) and vicariously (less painful). By Sunday morning, I had sent Tom an email with a brief outline of my proposal for a course to be called Learn from Failure. It would be from real life "cases" of high-profile failures and, through post-fact analysis or Monday-morning quarterbacking, my students and I would tease out the lessons to be learned from each. I have been teaching the course ever since.

As the course evolved, so did my thinking about failure and its drivers. I was given the opportunity to teach the course in the university's honors program. However, it had to be broader than a business course. I developed a hypothesis that failure in decision-making had the same fundamental causes in business, warfare, and developmental economics. From this thinking, more hypotheses emerged on specific drivers of failure and how we can cope with them. Over time, all these became the thesis upon which this book is based.

The book is descriptive. I explain in detail why we fail in decision-making with many examples from my own experiences as well as from high-profile failures (from Enron to AOL/Time Warner to RIM/Blackberry to Steve Ballmer/Microsoft and many others). I have reduced each of the factors driving failure to bullet point summaries at the end of each chapter to make it easy for the reader to cut to the chase.

As you read this book, you will have many moments where you will say to yourself, "Sure, I knew that." You will also have moments where you will say, "I never thought about it that way." And you will have those a-ha! moments. These are what I call BGOs, which stands for a "blinding glimpse of the obvious." When you've finished the book, you will have many insights into why you fail in decision-making and how you can improve your batting average. More importantly, you will have the knowledge necessary to learn from failure.

The book is also prescriptive. Following each driver of failure is a delineation of action steps to be taken to reduce or eliminate their impact. These steps are also summarized in bullet point fashion at the end of each chapter.

Many of the ideas herein come from the work of others. What is unique is how I have woven them together to create a fabric of personal design. Picasso said, "Good artists copy, but great artists steal." I've done my best to steal. I've woven anecdotes throughout the book to help make my points clearer as we tend to relate to and learn from the narrative. However, I must acknowledge the importance of the work of others in this book. Sir Isaac Newton said, "If I have seen further than other men, it is because I have stood on the shoulders of giants."

So why am I writing this book? In part, it's because many have told me I should. I also believe in the words of William Saroyan who said, "Good people are good because they've come to wisdom through failure. We get little wisdom from success, you know … One who doesn't try cannot fail and become wise." And lastly, I know that I would be disappointed in myself if I didn't. It would be a yes answer to the question, "Do you have any regrets?"

Why didn't I write it years ago? Ironically, I think it was because of the fear of failing. But a wise man once said that fearing failure is worse than failure itself. If you're afraid you're going to fail, you end up not trying.

As you read this book, you will see many areas where its elements are applicable beyond decision-making in business. My thesis proposes a new way for you to look at the entire process of making decisions. Marcel Proust once wrote, "The real voyage of discovery consists not in seeking new landscape, but in having new eyes." This book endeavors to give you Proust's "new eyes."

CHAPTER 1
IN THE BEGINNING

First, What Do I Mean by Failure?

"Fail early, fail often." That's the new mantra of Silicon Valley. Many venture capitalists won't finance an entrepreneur who hasn't failed at least once. So, why do I position failure so negatively? First, my singular focus is on decision-making. I define a decision as taking actions (or not acting) to bring a situation from the current state to some desired state. Not achieving that desired state is failure. It's that simple. Now, let's get on with the book.

My Story—My Failure

My first significant failure happened when I was just hitting my stride. Up to that point, failure happened to other people, not me. *Fail* was a four-letter word. I didn't get where I was by failing, and I certainly wouldn't get where I was going by failing.

I had taken a new job running a subsidiary of Citibank, aka Citigroup, based in Bogota, Colombia. It put me in the vortex of a shotgun wedding between my company and local investors. We had been forced to sell majority ownership to local investors by a government decree called *Colombianizacion* or "Colombianization" in English. We had to sell 51 percent, giving the local investors control.

As further background, these were the days of the "wild, wild west" in Colombia ('83–'86). All heads of major multinationals lived as if

1

we were kidnapping targets because, in principle—at any moment in time—we could be. So, I had armed guards, 24/7 at our fenced-in home and a safe haven built in the house with a short-wave radio to Citibank's security arm. I generally had no preset schedule, two offices and, unannounced, I would occasionally work from home.

I rotated cars, drivers, and routes to work, sat in the front with the driver, and sometimes drove while he sat beside me. I did everything except have lead and follow cars (conspicuous and costly), and I would not allow my driver to carry a gun. First, because in a kidnapping, the driver is the first one to be taken out, and second, I would rather have been kidnapped than shot.

Citibank paid for two security consultants, Mike Ackerman and Lou Polombo. They were ex-CIA and based in Miami. The core strategy we followed at their recommendation was to be a harder target than my colleagues who were high-profile heads of other multinationals. The theory was that, when a kidnapping was being planned, the kidnappers would stake out two or three targets and then choose the one who was the softest target. Ackerman and Polombo maintained that nobody was bulletproof. You just needed to be harder to hit than others around you. The head of Coca-Cola, who did have armed lead and chase cars, said he felt safer in Bogota than he did when he visited Coke headquarters in Atlanta, unaccompanied by his private army.

While I was living in Colombia, kidnapping touched my life twice. First, the father of the woman who ran operations for me, Ana de Vieco, was kidnapped. I will never forget the day she came in to my office and burst into tears as she told me what happened.

The second was when an executive of a multinational company was kidnapped. His behavioral patterns were too predictable, the makings of a soft target. When the multinational bought dollars for the ransom, they had to use the black market. My operations folks checked the bills to ensure they weren't counterfeit.

The icing on the cake was that Citibank would not disclose whether they would pay ransom or not. The policy was to not disclose this to anyone because if the answer were yes, and the word got out, that would heighten one's risk of being kidnapped. Comforting. So that's the backdrop for this story.

The local capital market was small, and the wealth in the country was concentrated. This meant Citi had to sell the shares to wealthy families. Call it arrogance or just a strong belief in our expertise; whatever it was, we were awful partners. We had no expertise in, or patience for, dealing with an uninitiated (into banking anyway), outside board of directors.

All this joint venture stuff fundamentally meant that, deep in the organization, at the operational level, outsiders could question what our management team had decided to do. We would have to justify our decisions to outsiders. Not only that, none of our partners knew our business. We struggled to cope with these outsiders questioning our decisions. It just was not part of our DNA. We were in more than one hundred countries, and we were minority partners in only two others. In both of those, we had bought our way into the minority position because of the attractiveness of the franchise and not sold ourselves down because we were forced to as in Colombia. Even though the ownership end result is the same, how you got there makes a big difference.

In choosing our partners, we carefully selected families with the finest reputations. They were also three families who had no previous business ties and were from different cities. That gave us some sense of comfort that the three were unlikely to band together against us. We believed there would always be one of the three we could bring to our side in a dispute.

On their side, they were delighted to have the opportunity to invest with a prestigious multinational. Our organization became a substantial player in the local markets with twenty-six branches spread across the country. Our shareholders recognized their limited knowledge of our business and agreed to us having the unilateral right to appoint one of our employees as the president of the company, while they maintained a veto never exercised. On all other matters, they had control. It was an uncomfortable and complex situation.

The Chinese have a saying about parties who sleep together with different dreams: the romance is unlikely to endure. Not long after I arrived, one of the three families sold out their interests. The buyer was a self-made man in the construction industry with a reputation for corrupt practices. Just putting the facts together (self-made man, construction industry), a prima facie case was made for an undesirable shareholder and partner, to say the least. Imagine saying no to that guy in the boardroom! Was he a version of Tony Soprano or was he just James Gandolfini playing a part? To our shareholders, the answer was clear. He was an unacceptable partner. Given the backdrop of the Colombian environment at that time, this was not an unreasonable conclusion for them to reach.

What was his agenda? Was he trying to legitimize his operations? Was he trying to climb the social ladder by sitting at the table with two of the finer families of the country and our organization as well? It was likely some combination of all three together with a nose for an opportunity for "green mail," meaning the purchase of enough shares in a firm to threaten the disruption of normal operations. This could force the purchase of the green mailer's shares back at a premium to end the disruption. Whatever his agenda was, there we were, blindsided.

Our local partners were outraged. They were highly respected families who traveled in the best of local society's circles. The new entrant did not enjoy such acceptance or legitimacy.

I tried to be pragmatic about the situation and actually met face-to-face with our new "partner." That was considered by most around me to be a horrible mistake. It was. I just wasn't smart enough to see it. It was an interesting experience in that he actually appeared to be a humble, respectful person who professed to only want to make a sound investment. Nobody was going to buy that one. Our other partners were in disbelief that I had met with him.

The "guidance" from head office was "Do something about it!" Yeah, right. Like what? Before I could develop much of a strategy, our initial partners approached the new entrant to buy him out. We were totally opposed as they had become too tightly linked over the years and would hold a controlling 51 percent interest. We risked losing management control. That was an anathema, and we told them so in no uncertain terms.

Nonetheless, they responded to the prospects of green mail by buying him out at an undisclosed price. I have no doubt he left with a big smile on his face. They announced the deal after the fact. My head office was outraged. They felt I had allowed the situation to get out of control. I had just had my first big professional failure.

Fortunately, my company had a strong risk-taking culture and was tolerant of failure. You may get put in the penalty box, but you could work your way out of it and get to play again. Clearly, I was in the penalty box and had to work my way out.

There is a saying in Spanish. "*Voy o van!*" This translates to "I go or they go." It's sort of a "Mexican standoff." At first, we pursued the "voy" side and attempted to sell our stake. With the help of some investment bankers, I searched for purchasers for our stake to no avail. Plan B was to find another local buyer for our local partners' shares. We had shifted from "voy" to "van." The purchaser would be the local archdiocese of the Catholic Church. Yes, that's right; one of the wealthiest entities in the country outside of the federal government was looking for an investment, and they found our firm attractive. The deal was struck—"subject to" a few conditions. I told the head office the problem was solved. They were ecstatic.

It was time for my scheduled home leave, so I made my annual trek to my vacation home in Vermont, leaving the lawyers to wrap up the details. I was going to pause and reflect on what had not happened thus far. Note there had been no substantive disagreements between our partners and us. The only exception was their buying out the other partner and thus concentrating ownership. Was this a genuine threat of a board takeover or just a posturing boogeyman? Were we wasting time and energy for nothing?

Shortly after I arrived in Vermont, I was walking across the street in Woodstock when a black cat crossed my path. I couldn't avoid it. I'm not superstitious, but I don't walk under ladders unless I have to. I will confess a chill ran down my spine.

A couple of days later, I got a call from our firm's local attorney. "You need to return at once." He would give no explanation—just that I needed to get back to Bogota. So, in the middle of my vacation in Vermont, I abandoned my family and returned. The situation seemed, and was, bizarre.

When I returned, I learned Roberto Calvi, the CEO of Banco Ambrosiano, and nicknamed "God's Banker," had hung himself from Blackfriar's Bridge in London in an apparent suicide on June 17, 1982.

His jacket pockets were stuffed with rocks but an article in the *Economist* said he would have had to be a circus acrobat to have managed to get into the position in which he was found. It was later judged to be a murder, but no one was ever convicted of the crime.

Banco Ambrosiano's main shareholder was the Vatican Bank. The scandal was huge and reached right up to Archbishop Paul Marcinkus, president of the Vatican's Bank. He was known as the "pope's banker." Banco Ambrosiano went bankrupt shortly after Calvi's death. The Catholic Church, in recognition of "moral involvement," later paid out $224 million to Ambrosiano's creditors.

The archdiocese, my counterparty, stopped returning my phone calls. Radio silence. They dropped out of sight without a word of explanation. I never heard from them even though I remained in the country for another year. My solution to the shareholder problem had failed.

What lessons could be learned from this? What were the things I could identify and never do again? Frankly, for a couple of decades, I didn't have a clue. It just seemed like I was a victim of circumstance; it was just bad luck. Sure, I deserved to be in the penalty box because it had happened on my watch. In fact, I was passed over for the next big promotion that should have been mine. But what could I learn from this? I had no idea. I got screwed, plain and simple.

As I proceed through the book, I'll keep coming back to the Colombian story to show how my concepts explain why my solutions to the shareholder problem failed. I will point out what specifically I could have—and should have—done to avoid failure. I will Monday-morning quarterback, applying the framework for analysis of failure that constitutes my thesis.

Another thing that makes learning from failure difficult is that decisions are mostly unique and different in important ways. There are times you can say, "I've seen this movie before," but those tend to be rare and, even then, the surrounding circumstances will be different simply because you are in a different time period and facing a different future. Seeing patterns that aren't real is more a risk of apparent but not real learning as will be discussed in a later chapter on instinctive decision-making.

Part of my thesis, as mentioned earlier, is to learn from failure, you must understand what causes it. What are the fundamental drivers of failure? What sort of framework will enable us to understand and learn from all failures in decision-making? That's what this book is about. If you put into practice everything recommended in this book, you will still fail—but you'll make better decisions and fail less frequently. As importantly, you'll be able to learn from your failures in a way that will enable you to continuously improve the quality of your decisions. Mahatma Gandhi said, "Those who know how to think need no teachers."

The Man in the Mirror
I'm starting with the man in the mirror,
I'm asking him to change his ways.
—Michael Jackson

To benefit from this book, you must be the "man in the mirror." Michael goes on to say, "If you wanna make the world a better place, take a look at yourself and then make a change." Yes, Michael's song was about making the world a better place, a laudable pursuit for sure, but we are on a much smaller mission. You want to be a better decision-maker. You want to beat the odds. If you think about his words in the context of becoming a better decision-maker, his message applies.

What do I mean by that—and why is it so important that I make it the subject of chapter 1? Because most of us, when confronting failure, play the blame game. Our reactions are something like: They were out to get me; my luck was bad; I depended on people who dropped the ball, etc. I once saw a bumper sticker that captured the thought well. "Errors have been made. Others will be blamed."

If one looks externally instead of internally, it mostly ends there with no internal growth or real insight. As mentioned, easy answers are quickly found: it was a bad break; I got screwed; others dropped the ball, and I took the fall; etc. These answers most often are at least partially true and so are both easy and comfortable to hold onto because the fault is external. It's a tough process to do the internal soul-searching required to identify the role we ourselves played in the failure. But therein lies the path to success and better decision-making in the future.

True introspection requires a heady combination of curiosity, courage, and inner strength. Holding oneself accountable and taking responsibility for failure is tough. It implies you could be part of the problem and that you might need to change, which are both scary prospects for most of us. We become emotional and don't consider what we might have done differently to achieve a more favorable outcome. That's the key. I repeat for emphasis, what *we* could have done differently to achieve a more favorable outcome. It comes down to the ability to be introspective.

Introspection is tough, but it must be practiced with great discipline to benefit from this book. To learn from failure, you need to understand what drives it—and you need to 'fess up to your role in it.

You cannot develop Marcel Proust's "new eyes" without both introspection and understanding the concepts of this book. Successfully applying the principles takes more than intelligence and understanding. It takes a lot of work and self-discipline. Many of us, because of ego, cannot master it. Denis Waitley said, "Failure should be our teacher, not our undertaker. Failure is delay, not defeat. It is a temporary detour, not a dead end. Failure is something we can avoid only by saying nothing, doing nothing, and being nothing."

Let's Not Build the Tower of Babel

They are one people and have one language, and nothing will
be withheld from them which they purpose to do.
Come, let us go down and confound their speech.
—Genesis 11:5–8

It's going to be important to embrace some new language in order for you to understand the concepts underpinning my thesis. After all, in surfing, there are almost two hundred terms specific to the sport, ranging from "getting air" to "wipeout" and including catchy terms like "goofy-footed." So, I think it's fair, given the seriousness of our voyage together, to get some language straight between us.

An old friend, Doug Smith (more about Doug later in the book) taught me that in managing change (remember Marcel Proust's "new eyes" mentioned in the preface?), your two scarcest resources are language and energy. None of the words will be entirely new to you, but they are likely to be defined in a narrow and precise way, more than you're accustomed to hearing. Most of these terms will be defined along the way, but a few need to be understood up front.

The first is failure itself. I defined it at the beginning of this chapter as not successfully changing a situation from its current state to some desired state. The second is decision-making. Decision-making is fundamentally about making the desired change happen, i.e. taking the situation one is confronted with from its current state to some desired state.

The third is strategy. A generic dictionary type definition of strategy would go something like this: "Strategy is an elaborate and systematic plan of action required to achieve goals that is extensively premeditated." A businessman would likely say something like: "Discovering and targeting attractive markets and then crafting positions that deliver sustainable competitive advantage."

Underlying these definitions is an assumption that the goals to be achieved are sound. Generally speaking, this book will operate under the assumption that the appropriate underlying goal is the maximization of stakeholders' value. Stakeholders, as the name implies, are any group that has a legitimate vested interest in the decision to be made. They may include investors, peers and superiors, employees, regulators, and society in general. Balancing these interests is crucial and at the heart of the decision itself.

The next term is complexity. It describes just how difficult the situations are that we confront when we make decisions. I'll discuss complexity using a range of terms going from simple to complicated to complex and finally to chaos. The degree of difficulty of effectively dealing with situations dramatically increases as we move from the simple to the complicated to the complex to the chaotic. I discuss the spectrum of complexity in some detail in chapter 3.

The fifth term is "mental model." We all have one. It's our idiosyncratic view of how the world works. To clarify, let me give you a couple of examples. Some of us see life as a chess game. It's both strategic (an evolving plan) and tactical (the next couple of moves). You must follow certain rules. A pawn can only move like this, and a knight can only move like that. There are winners and losers. Your objective is to be the winner.

Another mental model of life goes like this. Life is like surfing. There are no winners and losers. There are no set rules. Huge forces (ocean waves) that are totally out of your control can influence you dramatically. These forces can make you "bail" or enable you to "hang ten" even in "heavy" conditions.

Mental models adapt and adjust as we experience life. Our mental model consists of certain decision-making rules that guide us in making decisions. We then experience the real world and the outcome of our decisions. Do we like them or not? Based on the answer, we adjust our mental models. Whatever your mental model is of how life works today, the objective you've signed up for in reading this book is to modify your model by viewing life (decisions) with Proust's new eyes. This book will serve as a vicarious experience of life and decision-making. You will safely learn from the failure of others.

Finally, I need to explain how I use the terms management and leadership. This will be discussed at length in chapter 5. For now, suffice it to say that, while many use the terms interchangeably, I do not. Put simply, leadership is about vision, establishing values, the future, and change. Management is about execution, living values, today, and optimizing the status quo. While everyone in the organization leads and manages, the two activities are distinctly different. As you move up the hierarchy of your organization, the way you spend your time shifts toward leadership and away from management. This will become clearer as we move through the rest of the book.

It's Everywhere!

Ninety-nine point nine nine percent of all biological species which have ever existed are now extinct. Failure in this context is measured over hundreds of millions of years.
—Paul Ormerod[1]

No doubt failure is ubiquitous. Reading Ormerod's description of Mother Nature's track record was shocking to me. If Mother Nature

---

1. *Why Most Things Fail: Evolution, Extinction & Economics,"* Paul Omerod, prior head of the economic assessment unit of the *Economist*.

has this kind of failure rate, what makes us mere mortals think we should bat .1000 or even .500?

So, I did some digging. Ormerod said, "On a dramatically shorter time scale, more than 10 percent of all the companies in America disappear each year. Large and small, from corporate giants to the tiniest one-person business, they fail."

I dug further. I learned that of the hundred largest companies in the United States at the turn of the twentieth century, eighty-one were no longer on the list. They had either been acquired, gone bankrupt, or just weren't large enough to run with the big dogs.

I went on to do a thorough review of rather rigorous work done by some very smart people who examined, applying detailed research and robust business logic, success in the business world. Specifically, I focused on Tom Peters and Robert Waterman and their award-winning book, *In Search of Excellence.*

If we look at the thirty-two public companies that Peters and Waterman selected from numerous industries for their "excellence," fifteen of those companies underperformed the Dow Jones Industrial Average in the ensuing twenty years.[2] Of the seventeen that outperformed the Dow, only nine did so convincingly, i.e., with returns more than 3 percent higher than the Dow. The remaining eight were above the average by 3 percent or less, which is okay but hardly excellent.

Bear in mind these were companies chosen for their excellence in leadership and management. Peters and Waterman were not stock pickers or portfolio managers looking to outperform the Dow. They were writing on management excellence. That doesn't discredit their work in any way. In fact, it validates it.

My point is that those thirty-two public companies were excellent in 1982, but they got into trouble in varying degrees over the next twenty years and couldn't maintain their excellence.

I then went on to Jim Collins's *Good to Great: Why Some Companies Make the Leap and Others Don't,* which was written in 2001. Jim and his team of twenty-one research associates started with a base of 1,435 companies and sorted for the ones that had gone from mediocre

2. *In Search of Excellence,* Thomas J. Peters and Robert H. Waterman Jr., HarperCollins Publisher.

performance for ten years or more to outstanding performance over fifteen years. They read more than six thousand articles and generated more than two thousand pages of interview transcripts in what ended up being a five-year project. They found eleven companies that met their criteria.

Here's how they fared in the ten years after Collins's work was published:

1. Abbott Laboratories—Excellent—Stock up 25 percent versus Dow (10 percent).
2. Circuit City—Poor—Filed for Bankruptcy in 2009.
3. Fannie Mae— Poor—2008 bailout cost taxpayers about $300 billion.
4. Gillette—Good—Acquired by P & G in 2009.
5. Kimberly-Clark—Poor—Stock appreciation/dividends (5 percent p.a.) since 2000.
6. Kroger—Fair—10 percent stock appreciation equaled Dow.
7. Nucor— Excellent—Stock went from $15 to $45 in ten years.
8. Philip Morris—Mixed—Altria poor—PM International strong since 2008 spin-off.
9. Pitney Bowes—Poor—Stock down 45 percent over ten years.
10. Walgreens—Poor—Stock price flat for ten years.
11. Wells Fargo—Poor—Flat stock price for ten years.

Nine had fallen off the path of greatness—six of them precipitously. That's a pretty dramatic reversal of performance. Again, I don't at all believe that this discredits Collins's work, including his conclusions about the five common attributes of companies that make the leap. Quite the contrary. In most cases, the companies whose performance faltered failed to continue following Collins's prescription for success, which, ironically, was derived from the companies themselves. They failed because they were/are run by people who failed in decision-making, and it caught up with them.

Failure in decision-making has attracted much attention of late. McKinsey has provided substantial coverage of the topic. They conducted a survey of 2,207 executives regarding their perceptions of the quality of the decisions made by their company: 28 percent thought the "quality of decisions was generally good," 60 percent thought "bad decisions were about as frequent as good ones," and 12 per cent thought "good decisions were infrequent." That's a pretty poor track record. More than half of the executives thought they were wrong 50 percent of the time.

Keep in mind that this is a self-assessment where one might expect a bias toward the positive given the pride most executives feel about their organizations. After all, they run them. Thus, the quality of decisions made in business is substantially lower than we might expect. In terms of major strategic decisions and their track record of success, research has shown that 70–90 percent of mergers fail to deliver expected synergies and that the purchase price exceeds value more than 50 percent of the time.

But this book is about more than business decision failure. Government policy is basically trial and error. International development is fraught with failure. Just check out the track record of our international aid organization within the State Department, USAID. William Easterly, the economist and author of *The White Man's Burden*, provides a scathing review. In warfare, Helmuth von Moltke, a German military strategist, said, "No battle plan survives contact with the enemy." And in our personal lives, nobody said it better than poet Robert Burns: "The best-laid plans of mice and men / Often go awry."

So, you can see that failure is all around us. It happens to amateurs and experts, from the best and the brightest to mere mortals. It is inescapable. Given the ubiquity of failure, I was somewhat surprised to find when I began my personal "Proust journey" that most work done on understanding failure was in bits and pieces. The best comprehensive effort on the subject I found was Paul Ormerod's *Why Most Things Fail*. I have drawn on some of his concepts in the writing of this book. Ormerod's work is technically robust, but as the title suggests, it focuses on why "things" fail as opposed to why decisions lead to failure.

More recently, the *McKinsey Quarterly* has published some work on biases of decision-makers as drivers of failure, which I have used extensively in chapter 2. Also, the *Harvard Business Review* devoted an entire issue (April 2011) to the subject (cited in chapter 4). Most recently, *Harvard Business Review* devoted another entire issue (summer 2012) to managing uncertainty. I also draw from this issue in chapter 4. Again, this work describes part of the problems we encounter in decision-making—not the whole problem as this book endeavors to do.

The focus of this book is to present a comprehensive understanding of why decisions frequently fail and learn to use those insights in the development of methods to beat the odds and make sounder decisions.

Sum and Substance

Nothing is perfect. Life is messy. Relationships are complex.
Outcomes are uncertain. People are irrational.
—Hugh Mackay, social researcher

Mackay nailed it. That's part of the reason it's so difficult to learn from failure. Just like my example in chapter 1 with my multinational employer and local shareholders, even when you separate historical events and see clear cause and effect, situations are so full of idiosyncratic risk that there generally aren't any clear patterns from which to learn. A framework is needed on which we can hang the facts of a situation in an orderly fashion that makes patterns and lessons clear.

After experiencing, observing, studying, teaching, and learning about failure for many years, I have developed various hypotheses about what drives failure. These have been distilled down to a thesis. The thesis is built around a view of the environment that surrounds us when we make decisions and the key skills or fitness levels we bring to the challenge of making successful decisions.

I describe the environment as being composed of irrationality (of decision-makers), complexity (of the situations we face), and uncertainty (of what lies ahead out of our control). To this environment we bring certain skills and qualities that include leadership, management, and oversight. I put these into a framework I call the "Cube."

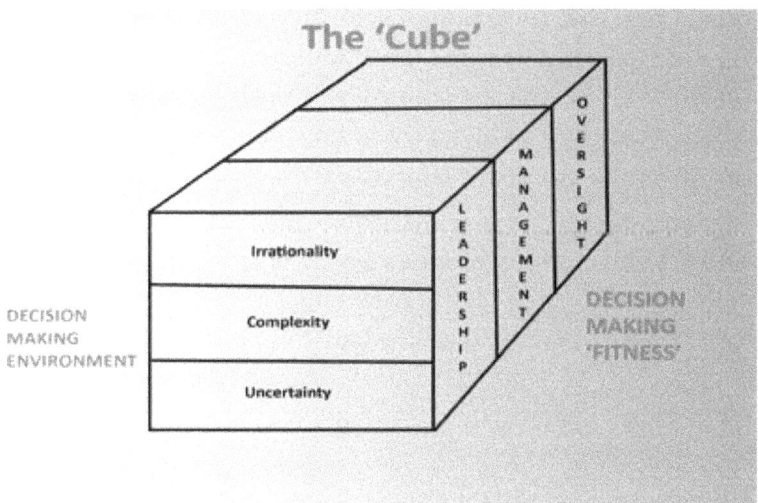

Note these *fitness* characteristics can apply to the organization addressing a decision or to an individual decision-maker. Into this Cube, I put all the facts and circumstances of a particular failed decision and its outcomes and perform a post-fact analysis. From this process, the lessons of the failure emerge.

The book is divided into four parts mirroring the Cube: irrationality, complexity, uncertainty, and the fitness landscape, which consists of leadership management and oversight. In each part, I explain the underlying concept and apply my opening story to show how it applies. I also add personal vignettes and other examples to further drive home the lessons learned.

Irrationality covers the behavior of decision-makers and those who surround them, their humanness, and their biases. Complexity describes the nature of the messy world in which we live in a highly structured way that is meant to help us understand and deal with it more effectively. Uncertainty speaks to the contention that all decisions, either explicitly or implicitly, contain a forecast of the future that cannot be known.

In the fitness landscape, I look at the skills and abilities we bring to the decision-making process that help us deal with irrationality, complexity, and uncertainty. I define leadership and management by comparing and contrasting them. My contention is that, while leaders manage and managers lead, leadership and management are fundamentally different. I then turn to oversight (mentors, boards of directors, regulators, auditors, etc.) and discuss what it brings to the process and how and why it is critically important.

Weakness in any of the three skills can—and generally will—lead to failure. Luck can save you, but generally it won't. While this book is fundamentally about decision-making in business, as mentioned earlier, I've developed my thesis by studying warfare and development economics. Also, through my years of interacting with students on the subject, I have come to believe it applies to almost any area of decision-making, including our personal lives.

CHAPTER 2
IRRATIONALITY: WE DON'T THINK THE WAY WE THINK WE THINK

Your reason and your passion are the rudder and the sails of your seafaring soul. If either your sails or your rudder be broken, you can but toss and drift, or else be held at a standstill in mid-seas.
For reason, ruling alone, is a force confining; and passion, unattended, is a flame that burns to its own destruction.
—Khalil Gibran, On Reason and Passion

The problem we face in decision-making is that all too often "passion, unattended, is a flame that burns to its own destruction." Passion leads to irrationality with all the negative consequences that Gibran describes. I would extend Gibran's statement to say, *emotions* in general, instead of limiting it to *passion* as you will see in this chapter.

A good way to start understanding irrationality is to define rationality. Some standard dictionary definitions include: consistent with or based on reason, logical, and having its source in or guided by the intellect.

Classic economics teaches as *Homo economicus* (economic man), we behave in ways that are both rational and in our self-interest. As consumers, therefore, we endeavor to maximize utility and, as producers, we maximize economic profit. Decisions are made logically and rationally, carefully weighing costs and benefits to maximize self-benefit. Economic man is intelligent, analytical, and has perfect self-control in the pursuit of his future goals. Emotions play no role in the process. In other words, *Homo economicus* exists only in the minds, textbooks, and models of classical economists. None of us actually operates this way.

Fortunately, much work has been done recently in the area of behavioral economics where empirical analysis of actual behavior is the cornerstone of analysis rather than unrealistic ideals. I draw on that work in the sections that follow.

We're all taught the importance of being rational in making decisions, and we're taught how to do it. The teaching ranges from making a pros and cons list to complex analytical techniques in critical thinking, strategic assessment frameworks, economics, math, science, and finance. As products of our education, we believe we are rational in making decisions when nothing could be further from the truth because none of this takes our humanness into account. We are emotional creatures with biases, flaws, and limitations that dramatically compromise the underlying assumptions in this line of thinking. This chapter discusses how we really think versus how we *think* we think.

How Not to Do an Acquisition

If you can keep your wits about you while all others are losing theirs, and blaming you. The world will be yours and everything in it, what's more, you'll be a man, my son.
—*Rudyard Kipling*

In business, I think one of the most fertile areas for discussion of irrationality is the acquisition. Given the importance of the decision and the level in the organization at which these decisions are made, one would think the logic, intellectual firepower, and highly disciplined thinking would be at the pinnacle of rationality. Nothing could be further from the truth.

For starters, it's important to understand the underlying rationale of an acquisition is that one and one is going to equal three. If it's two or less, it's a loser. I already mentioned 70 percent of all acquisitions fail. Here's part of the reason.

What follows is a story of a real acquisition decision that I was a part of. Like all acquisitions, it was potentially a profitable deal provided you don't overpay.

I was the chief financial officer (CFO) of the potential acquirer. My boss, Pete, was a smart guy with a heart as big as the outdoors. He was also tough as nails, a straight shooter, and a transparent guy. You always knew where you stood with him.

This was a time when many financial institutions were in trouble and were hiving off businesses to raise capital. We were active bidders but, so far, with no success. This meant watching our competitors gain scale, which is never a good thing.

As CFO, my staff orchestrated the development of the bids. We got all the required assumptions from the functional experts in treasury, marketing, credit, and operations. We ran these through our model to develop a range for the premium we could pay and still have an attractive deal. This was all scientific in theory, but it was loaded with malleable assumptions. If you didn't like the model's outcome, just change the assumptions, within reason of course.

All this data was put in a binder that represented the analytical foundation for determining our final bid. But this disciplined and analytically robust process yielded bids consistently too low to win.

There was a feeding frenzy. I didn't think the premiums being paid were justifiable. But the word was spreading around the company that "we didn't have the *cojones* to pull the trigger." I couldn't help but note our assumptions for the model had been getting increasingly aggressive. We were like a dog chasing its tail.

And then a big fish came along: $2 billion in assets. The process quickly distilled down to two serious bidders, and we were one. The only question was what premium would we pay over the $2 billion in assets.

The binder contained many scenarios with premiums ranging from $100 million to $125 million. My boss and I reviewed it with the rest of his staff in detail. We were ready, though my gut told me the binder's scenarios had been biased by everyone's desire to win and show the rest of the organization we had what it takes. In other words, I thought

$125 million was aggressive.

The call came to meet in the big boss's office. The group included him, John, Pete, Tony (John's right hand man for acquisitions), and me. With my copy of the binder under my arm, Pete and I paraded up to John's office. The pleasantries lasted under a minute.

John asked "Bob, what's your number?" He was referring to the premium.

I had a moment of internal panic because I was expecting a rigorous discussion of the scenarios in the binder and the range of premiums. It became abruptly evident that wasn't going to happen. The message was clear. Just give me your number.

My mind raced as I thought through the scenarios. I was asked for a single number and not a narrative.

I did my best not to blink, and after a brief pause, I said, "$125 million." Compared to our past bids, this was literally starting at the top. I wanted to win too. The bid now contained an accumulation of biases: mine, my staff, and the rest of the organization involved in the process. And these biases compounded.

John turned to my boss and asked, "Pete?"

Pete didn't blink either. He said, "$150 million." I tried to keep my best poker face though I admit I'm usually pretty transparent. I had no idea whatsoever where Pete got that number. We had not discussed anything beyond $125 million.

John knew Pete well, and Pete, being Pete, was totally transparent. Also, I knew that John had reviewed the binder thoroughly. He was the most buttoned-up and unemotionally analytical executive I'd ever known.

John asked Pete, "Where did you get that number?"

Pete immediately replied, "I made it up. I want to win." That took my breath away. Pete was a very competitive guy. We all were or we wouldn't have reached positions that brought us into that room. But this seemed over the top.

John turned and said, "Tony?"

Tony had been around the block many times. He was one of those guys who had seen it all and done it all. Tony didn't hesitate. He said, "John, it's whatever you want it to be."

I thought to myself, *This is a classic Wall Street dick-stretching contest.*

Tony said, "This $2 billion of assets will get mixed in with the rest of our businesses, and no one will know how well it performs going forward. If you think it's strategically important, then go for it. Whatever it takes." This was to be my first lesson that whenever an action is justified solely on "strategic importance" with no analysis behind it, you are on the road to perdition.

The room was still.

John picked up the phone and asked his assistant to get the acquiree's chairman on the phone. It took a matter of seconds for the call to go through. After ten seconds of pleasantries, John said, "So on the acquisition, what docs it take to be preemptive?" We only heard one side of the call, but the response clearly was, "Let me get back to you."

We all understood John wanted to know the premium they would accept to take this out of a bidding competition. Nobody said a word for what seemed like an eternity. The phone rang. John answered. It was the chairman. John listened and then said, "$180 million? Done." And that was it.

The acquisition proved to be a disaster. Contrary to what Tony said, our financial system enabled us to segregate this business and measure its performance separate from our overall performance. This information did not get outside of our inner circle, but, nonetheless, the numbers were there to show that, because the recession was worse than most everybody anticipated, the performance was nothing short of horrific. I stopped making the estimations of value when the number dropped below $80 million.

What went wrong in the acquisition? Here, the irrationality of the decision-makers is pretty clear. Gibran's sails overcame the rudder. In a subsequent section, I will dissect the irrationality to get a clearer understanding of what went wrong and provide some insights into how it might have been made more rational.

I give this as an example because I was there. But history is rife with examples as bad or worse than the one I described. There was a joke on Wall Street, where some of the best dark humor is ginned up. The joke described the two best positions to be in were to own any business during the eighties that either Citibank or American Express wanted to buy or to want to buy any business in the nineties that either of the two wanted to sell. The bid/offered spreads on the trades were huge. While American Express's fiascos were public (E. F. Hutton), Citibank's were smaller and less public. In the aggregate, they likely destroyed as much shareholder value or more.

The AOL/Time Warner merger is legendary and widely regarded as the worst deal of its kind in history. Steve Case and Jerry Levine had a dream. It was a brilliant dream, but there was no bridge between the dream and the reality of execution of a deal: between signing a deal and making the deal deliver value. To think the cultures of AOL and Time Warner could synergistically interact and create revenue that either of the two couldn't create on their own, or realize cost savings by sharing infrastructure, was a pipe dream. As Thomas Edison said, "Vision without execution is hallucination."

The fact was that Time and Warner had not successfully merged. The West Coast Warner movie guys couldn't stand the "white shoe" publishing guys in New York. And try putting into this mix Ted Turner's Turner Broadcasting System (CNN et al.). Nobody shared anything with anybody. As Donnie Brasco would say, "Forget about it." Even Turner quit the board in 2003.

How about News Corp's acquisition of MySpace for $585 million in 2005 and subsequent sale for $35 million six years later? What was Rupert Murdoch thinking? Did he believe his successful track record in buying traditional media companies would hold him in good stead in the purchase of a social media business? Worse still, did he feel MySpace would flourish under the management umbrella of a staid, old, traditional media company? Seriously, Rupert. What were you thinking? Whatever it was, certainly it wasn't rational.

And then there's Bank of America's acquisition of the mortgage originator Countrywide, which was later referred to as the worst deal in the history of the financial-services industry. A purchase price of $2.5 billion was followed by $40 billion in losses.

One of my favorites is the Kmart/Sears $11 billion deal. Sears's revenue dropped by 10 percent over next several years, and private investor/CEO Eddie Lambert (supposedly smart money) was deemed the worst CEO of the year in 2007 by the *New York Times*. The stock price has declined from $190 around the time of the acquisition/merger to about $8.65 in August of 2017. Nice job, Eddie.

No story about failed acquisitions would be complete without mentioning Daimler-Benz's purchase of Chrysler in 1998 for $36 billion. Chrysler's down-market focus on middle-income customers as compared to the Daimler-Benz focus on the upscale market segment led to such a disaster that Daimler-Benz actually paid $650 million to Cerberus Capital Management to take Chrysler off its hands.

Clearly, the list could go on and on. While I wasn't there to witness each incident, I'm confident that there was plenty of irrationality in the decision-making process for all these deals. Jack Welch had a name for the phenomenon: *deal heat*. You saw it in the deal I was a part of. It's one of a few reasons acquisitions fail (along with flawed strategy and failed integration of the two companies due principally to culture clashes). As mentioned at the start of this section, acquisitions are one of the most fertile areas for discussion of irrationality.

Consult Your Shrink before You Decide

The voice of the intellect is a soft one, but it does not rest
until it has gained a hearing.
—Sigmund Freud

McKinsey did a study that showed executives perceive their decision-making to be surprisingly weak. Citing the development of a field called *behavioral economics*, they describe the negative impact of biases on decision-making.

One of the more interesting elements of their work pointed out that, while strategists work hard to consciously account for the psychology of others in marketing and other fields of business, they rarely account for their own biases when making decisions. I think part of this goes back to the way we are educated in business or other fields.

As previously mentioned, there is such an emphasis on logic, critical thinking, and being guided by the intellect that we naturally enter the workforce (life) believing that is the way people actually make decisions. Increasingly, empirical evidence is emerging that demonstrates that is not the case. The good news is there is also an increasing body of empirical evidence that applying various processes to de-bias decision-making can significantly enhance the quality of decisions. More on that later.

The bias categories described below loosely link to the cited work of Lovallo and Sibony. I also provide links back to the narratives I have previously discussed.

Ready, fire, aim: Action-oriented biases cause us to act faster than we should and without appropriate consideration of logic and sound analytics. Self-confidence is a necessary attribute in business but, pushed too far, it can easily lead to overconfidence and, in turn, to arrogance. When that happens, we push assumptions beyond reasonableness.

Citibankers were notorious for this. Most of us had a sense we could go where others had failed and could consistently operate at the edge of the envelope without falling into the abyss. This led to many failed acquisitions. Returning to the acquisition I described earlier, overconfidence and overoptimism were most certainly at play. A bias for action was clear.

Most studies show acquisitions generally fail to deliver shareholder value in line with expectations as previously noted. There are fundamentally two reasons: overpayment (deal heat) and an overestimation of the managerial ability to deal with cultural differences between the two companies.

Both of these issues are linked to overconfidence and, at the extreme, arrogance. They arise from the personality and character traits of the decision-maker and are dangerous weaknesses because they are invisible to them. These weaknesses cause them to believe they can manage newly acquired companies better than current management, magically, with little or no consideration of the problems that will be encountered. These biases cause them to disregard bad things that might happen and only focus on the good things. Over-optimism leads to poor assumptions that go beyond reason.

In the case of the Bogota story at the beginning of the book and the associated deal with the Catholic Church, my overconfidence and overoptimism abounded. I was managing up and basking in the glory of victory well before the game was over. A bias for action, overconfidence, and overoptimism resulted in my not taking the time to develop a plan B.

Ready, aim, aim, aim: The opposite of these action-oriented biases are stability biases. Analysis paralysis and fear of change will cause us to fail to act when action should be taken. People naturally resist change, and inertia takes over. There is great comfort in the status quo and a certain amount of self-gratification in anchoring ourselves to the path we are on. We focus on incremental improvement as our key challenge and ignore opportunities that would take us out of our comfort zones. Our human reaction to uncertainty is at the heart of these biases.

Stability biases come in various shapes and sizes. Throwing good money after bad, called the *sunk-cost fallacy* is another one. Often, we stick with our decisions in the face of clear evidence the dog won't hunt. In one of the entrepreneurial endeavors where I worked, the core business proposition was fatally flawed after $24 million of a $40 million investment had been spent. The venture capitalists who had invested in the business pushed the management team to morph the business in some viable, new direction. "You're smart guys. Figure something out." This resulted in expending another $8 million before we finally shut the doors.

Another stability bias (not mentioned by Lovallo and Sibony) is fear of failure. As I mentioned in the preface, fear of failure is worse than failure itself as it tends to develop the habit of not trying. Unwillingness to take risks in a fast-changing world is, in the long run, more dangerous than taking risks. If you have any doubts about this, go back to chapter 1 and check out some companies whose performance has faltered. Mary Pickford said, "If you have made mistakes, there is always another chance for you. You may have a fresh start any moment you choose, for this thing we call 'failure' is not the falling down, but the staying down."

Subtler, but still important, is that we naturally feel the negative consequences of losses more than we do gains. As an example, studies have shown that, of two individuals who have enjoyed the same gain in their investment portfolio over some period, the one who does not check its performance regularly but only at the end of the period will be much happier with their return. Seeing it go down in the short run has greater negative impact than seeing it rebound has positive impact. This makes us more risk averse than we would otherwise be.

Conflict of interest: All too often, the interests of the decision-maker conflict with the interests of the firm, particularly the long-term interests of the firm. These interest biases often involve misaligned incentives. These are poorly structured compensation schemes that motivate delivering self-serving short-term results at the expense of the longer-term health of the firm.

A clear example of this issue is the bonus schemes on Wall Street leading up to the global financial crisis. The short-term focus of these bonus schemes drove behavior all along the mortgage generation and distribution chain, from mortgage brokers through to Wall Street investment bankers, to have a short-term, instant gratification attitude toward their jobs. It was not quite pump and dump, but it was close enough.

Here, the value of mortgage-backed securities was pumped, and then the securities were dumped by selling the securities as quickly as possible. Then on to the next deal. And investors' appetite for this paper seemed limitless.

While pump and dump is an amusing name, the activity it describes caused the global economy to tank for a perilously long period. It also put the financial institutions, where these people worked, in serious jeopardy. In turn, it jeopardized the long-term employment opportunities of the pumpers and dumpers.

Misaligned incentives also include the decision-maker's self-serving interest in their own unit in the organization. While we all know that successful businesses need to be run as integrated entities, human nature perniciously causes some level of silo mentality to creep into most all organizations. In vying for scarce resources (budgeting, bonus pools, staff count allocations, etc.), unit heads' views on many, many decisions are colored by self-interest. Everybody talks a good story about the good of the whole, but if you listen carefully, you will hear perspectives on discussions that reflect positions in the organizations.

Where you stand in life depends on where you sit. Of course, one is expected by superiors, peers, and subordinates to be a champion for their part of the organization. Nonetheless, this represents a bias that needs to be considered a possible compromise to rationality because unit interests are often in conflict with the interests of the firm.

Interest biases also include emotional attachments or agendas lodged in the subconscious of the decision-maker. People become attached to ideas—their own and others. They also reject them because they were "not invented here." This type of bias is idiosyncratic with no sustainable rationale to support it. It extends to products, people (loyalty), and—more broadly speaking—perceptions of the firm's goals.

Misperceiving the firm's goals is the last area of interest biases. The best example of this phenomenon is the maniacal focus on short-term earnings of executives of publicly held companies. This is another type of short-term focus. The question it entails is maximizing quarterly earnings to the detriment of the long-term prospects of the firm.

The consequences of this behavior have been recently demonstrated in the research project quoted below:

Companies deliver superior results when executives manage for long-term value creation and resist pressure from analysts and investors to focus excessively on meeting Wall Street's quarterly earnings expectations. This has long seemed intuitively true to us. We've seen companies including Unilever, AT&T, and Amazon succeed by sticking resolutely to a long-term view.[3]

While this is intuitive, it is comforting to get some real data, as provided by these researchers, that supports the intuition. Here's a snapshot of how the survey was conducted (performance data was tracked on 615 nonfinancial companies over fourteen years):

- These were large companies representing more than 60 percent of total US stock market capitalization.
- Various proxies were used to determine long-term thinking versus short-term thinking.
- Two examples are ratio of capital expenditures to depreciation

3   "Finally, Evidence that Managing for the Long Term Pays Off," Dominic Barton, James Manyika, and Sarah Keohane Williamson, *Harvard Business Review*, February 7, 2017.

and accruals as percentage of revenue.
- Comparisons were made with industry peers.
- 167 or about 27 percent were judged to have a long-term orientation.

Here is a summary of the indexed performance results of long-term versus short-term oriented companies:

- Average company revenue—47 percent higher.
- Average company earnings—36 percent higher.
- Average market capitalization—58 percent higher.

I find those numbers to be a compelling indication that managing for the long term is in the best interests of shareholders, yet 61 percent of executives and directors surveyed said they would cut discretionary spending to meet short-term forecasts.

Social Biases: These "arise from the preference for harmony over conflict." There are two categories of these according to Lovallo and Sibony: sunflower management and groupthink. Sunflower management is simply learning what bosses want and giving it to them or agreeing with them.

There's a saying in business that, loosely paraphrased, goes like this. If you have somebody working for you who thinks like you do, one of you is redundant. It's funny but true. Sunflower management adds no value, and it invites a lemminglike atmosphere in the work environment. Smart people hire for diverse thinking, encourage an environment of lively discussion and debate, welcome dissent and disagreement, and work toward consensus.

Our second social bias is *groupthink*. Research psychologist Irving Janus coined the term in his seminal work, *Groupthink: Psychological Studies of Fiascoes*. Since that time, the word has become so commonplace that its impact on decision-making is underestimated.

Groupthink is insidious as it, all too often, creeps into the decision-making process, crowding out the exploration of divergent views, crushing healthy disagreement and dissent, and preventing the analysis and evaluation of competing ideas. It is a rush to consensus that might be due to laziness (candor and dissent take both courage and energy), but most often, it occurs because of a "go-along-to-get-along" attitude that creeps into a group's decision-making process.

Pattern-Recognition Biases: Recognizing patterns and using that recognition in one's decision-making process is a natural, normal and healthy thing to do in decision-making—up to a point. Just like the difference between self-confidence and overconfidence, pattern recognition has important constraints that, if not followed carefully, can lead to failure in decision-making.

Confirmation bias, or reinforcement, describes our tendency to seek out only evidence that supports the decision we are leaning toward or already support while ignoring evidence to the contrary. A study was run at Stanford University where two equally sized groups of people were formed, one believing that capital punishment was a deterrent and the other believing it was not. Both groups believed that credible research supported their position.

Each group was given two research studies; one study showed it was a deterrent, and the other showed it was not. They were described as randomly selected. One would expect that, after the exposure to this research, participants would have been left in, more or less, the same position as before—perhaps having even moderated their views after exposure to this balanced research. That's not what happened.

After being exposed to this balanced research, people's views on their position sharpened and became more extreme. Further, when asked to describe the two pieces of research they were given, each side described research supporting their position as highly credible and authoritative while denigrating the work that opposed their view.

Without getting into politics, I am an avid viewer of CNN. I most certainly do not regard it as "fake news" as President Trump describes it. However, to combat my own confirmation bias, I go out of my way to watch Fox News. Doing this is hard work, but if one is serious about combating confirmation bias, that is the type of thing one must do.

The next type of pattern-recognition bias is the *false analogy* or *misleading experience*. I already mentioned the News Corp acquisition of MySpace. Murdoch's well-established track record as a successful acquirer of traditional news media companies undoubtedly influenced him into thinking he would also be a successful acquirer of a social media company. Wrong!

When MySpace was brought into the News Corp family, it was stifled and asphyxiated by the News Corp corporate bureaucracy and press for short-term earnings. While Myspace tried to monetize its user base way too early, Facebook's Mark Zuckerberg brilliantly built market share and staved off investors' appetite for revenue until he dominated the market and had successfully buried MySpace. The outcome of Murdoch's acquisition of MySpace was a blunder of epic proportions as previously described.

Another pattern-recognition bias is the *champion bias*. To get things done in most organizations, you need a champion. We all know that. The problem is we all too often forget the champion is naturally highly biased toward their project. We compound this by judging the attractiveness of the project based on the track record of the champion. Not smart. Keep your eye on the merits of the project and don't be distracted by the merits of the presenter.

The last pattern-recognition bias is the *recency bias*. Many of us seem to share the notion that the past six months of our lives will be repeated in large part in the next six months and beyond. That's rarely the case, but human nature would have us believe otherwise. We need to understand this bias is there and manage our way around and through it when required lest we enter a decision with a distorted view of the future.

Flawed Information: "Say what you have to say, not what you ought. Any truth is better than make-believe." Thoreau makes my point succinctly and clearly. The people around us can be a great asset, but it takes considerable work for that to happen. Without discipline and a tight decision-making process, they are far more likely to be a great liability. All too often, it is hard to tell the difference. I will start with the liability aspects and save the asset part for the discussion of how to substantially reduce the impact of irrationality in decision-making.

On the negative side, decision influencers can fail to bring value to the process, and in so doing, they are wasting time and resources. Decision influencers who seek consensus among themselves to avoid conflict and discomfort deny the decision-maker of the benefit of their best thinking. In other words, they are not earning their keep. Team consensus is critically important as a decision begins implementation.

Before that, when a decision is in the processing stage, candor, respectful conflict and criticism are both healthy and necessary. Otherwise, groupthink can feed into confirmation bias that I already discussed. So, there is added risk of failure with groupthink because the decision-makers' biases run rampant with no pushback. Even more dangerous is managing up where subordinates simply tell the boss what they think the boss wants to hear.

Weak subordinates or subordinates who are competent yet think the same way you do bring no substantive value to your decision-making process. The story told earlier of the credit card portfolio acquisition is a classic example of all these phenomena converging to create a horrendous blunder.

And then there is the bullshitter. We all know there are a lot of them out there. It may be hard to believe, but there is actually a professor emeritus at Princeton who has written a book entitled *On Bullshit*. His name is Dr. Harry Frankfurt. The book is a quick read and makes some interesting and worthwhile points. The first is the distinction between liars and bullshitters.

As Dr. Frankfurt describes it, liars know the truth (or think they do) and seek to mask it for their own reasons. But the truth is important to a liar since, to effectively manipulate it, he must know what it is.

The bullshitter is different. The bullshitter not only does not know the truth—the bullshitter couldn't care less about it. Like the liar, the bullshitter has a personal agenda. But the bullshitter spins their story to accomplish their agenda irrespective of the truth. Since the bullshitter believes their agenda is correct and they are not purposefully deceiving, the bullshitter feels they stand on higher moral ground than the liar.

Chronic bullshitters and compulsive liars are typically sorted out pretty early in their careers. It is the occasional offender who presents the problem. They are harder to spot and generally resort to their evil ways in times of duress and often when the stakes are high. This makes the consequences of their actions serious.

If both provide misinformation to the decision-making process, why is the distinction important? Because we do not treat bullshitters the same as we do liars—even though they both present important dangers to decision-making because of the misinformation they provide.

Liars are despicable creatures. Most of us consider them to be unethical and treat them accordingly. On-the-spot firing is appropriate in my view. Ethics are learned (or not) by the age of twenty, or should be. I never felt I was in the business of teaching ethics. There are moms and dads and priests, ministers, and rabbis to help people who have ethics issues.

My first experience firing someone was over a breach of ethics. He lied to me about a client breach of loan agreement covenants. After a brief conversation with my boss to ensure my bases were covered, he was fired on the spot. I hate firing people. I know it is painful for them and disruptive to their lives. Firing a liar however doesn't bother me at all.

Bullshitters however are generally treated lightly, particularly if they have redeeming qualities. Charismatic, witty bullshitters are often found to be charming. They are casually dismissed. "Oh, he's just bullshitting you."

In Frankfurt's book, he tells an anecdote of a father addressing his son on his deathbed. The father advises the son, "Never lie when you can bullshit your way out of it." The rationale behind the advice is simple. The consequences of bullshitting are dramatically less, though the impact on the quality of information provided to decision-makers is no less damaging.

Are bullshitters easier to spot than liars? Not the good ones. And worse still, there are probably more of them in business than there are liars though I don't know of any research on the subject.

In decision-making, both lies and bullshit are dangerous sources of misinformation. While I don't believe in second chances for liars, it may be appropriate to give one to a bullshitter. Here's one example. It was budget time, and the manager of our most profitable country was presenting his plan. This guy was generally considered one of our best managers with a long track record of beating his budget year after year by a considerable margin. I thought he was a sandbagger.

So, in the middle of his review, I laid out the facts as I saw them. I said, "Steve, you consistently budget year-over-year growth in earnings of 10–12 percent, and you deliver 20–25 percent. Your proposed budget of 11 percent growth is not good enough. You are depriving us of the benefit of your best thinking on what the business can actually do and distorting the budget process for the firm. I want a number that has got an 80 percent probability of being accomplished. No higher. I think that number is 22 percent. What do you think?" My reputation as a no-nonsense CFO was established.

Everyone in the room was stunned except my boss who thought it was great. Steve's boss later told me that I couldn't treat Steve that way because he delivered results. He didn't get it either.

I don't know if there is a correlation between bullshitters becoming liars, but they both certainly cross the ethics line. However, if every business manager that sandbagged in a budget review was called out as a bullshitter and fired, there would be many unfilled business manager positions.

Not only do I have a weak track record in dealing harshly with bullshitters, I must confess to having been one myself. Here's an example. As the CFO of a financial-services firm, I was making a presentation to the board of directors. My key point was that the return on equity, a key performance indicator, had improved considerably over the prior year.

The chairman of the board asked about another number on my slide, the return on assets, which had deteriorated.

I immediately replied, "That's not the important indicator. The ROE is where we should focus."

The chairman said, "Bob, if you put a number on a slide, I assume it's important. The ROA is there, and it has deteriorated. Obviously, a financial institution can improve its ROE by increasing leverage, deteriorating their ROA, and taking on greater financial risk."

He had me. I hesitated only for a moment and said, "You're right. I screwed up." He called me on it, and I learned my lesson. I survived the incident and later got promoted—twice. Depending on the situation, bullshitters likely should be given a second chance, but they need to be called out for their behavior as the chairman called me out.

Loosely linked to bullshitters but in a category by themselves are champions. They need to be considered separately from bullshitters because decision-makers create them. They are created because they are necessary to drive initiatives through the organization. However, we must always recognize them as being, by their nature, biased. They have a clear agenda that we must take into account when we assess their recommendations.

Trusting your gut: Another critically important source of bias in decision-making is instinctive or intuitive decision-making. Most of us have been advised at one time or another to follow our instincts, so it probably seems counterintuitive to be cautioned about doing so.

Experts say that instinctive decision-making can be useful—but only in limited circumstances. Daniel Kahneman, the only psychologist to win the Nobel Prize in Economics, described two modes of thinking as System 1 and System 2. System 1 is fast, involuntary, operates almost effortlessly, and is from our experience. It is instinctive. System 2 is slower, more deliberate, reflective, analytical, and requires conscious effort. Both systems are operating all the time. When we think of ourselves, we think in terms of System 2. But Kahneman's thesis is built around the thought that System 1 dominates our thought processes. His thesis is that this is an important danger in decision-making.

Gary Klein, also a psychologist, has a more expansive view of the applicability of instinctive decision-making, though both agree the limitations are substantial. In the referenced article, they endeavor to define the boundaries separating intuitive skill from biases like overconfidence.

Not surprisingly, it all boils down to the predictability of the environment surrounding the decision. Why is this not surprising? Simply because we know the foundation of instinctive decision-making is pattern recognition. Our subjective assessment of the applicability of the environment is insufficient. There are two key reasons why not, and both come from the work of Kahneman. First, all too often, we see patterns that do not apply to the situation at hand. Important decisions tend to be unique. Each has its own set of circumstances that do not generally match prior experiences. The more complex the decision is, the more likely this is to be true.

Categorization is particularly dangerous. All acquisitions are not alike. Nor are all new product launches or outsourcing decisions. Besides the problem of inapplicable patterns, when we make decisions under pressure, we resort to heuristics, or rules of thumb, to carry us through. These shortcuts get us into trouble because we think fast when we should be thinking slow.

Here is a case study to illustrate the dangers of instinctive decision-making. In 1991, two consultants, Rich Fairbank and Nigel Morris, had an idea for the credit card business. They believed that the data stored by credit bureaus was sufficiently robust to allow the categorization of borrowers by levels of risk and probability of payment default. They argued that this would enable credit card issuers to tier price and have multiple business models where the best customers would be rewarded with the lowest borrowing rates but would still be profitable because the expense of their credit losses would be lower.

While today, this seems obvious, in 1991, this was revolutionary thinking. At that time, all credit card issuers charged 19.8 percent APR, and all cards carried a $25 fee. There were no rewards programs.

Rich and Nigel shopped their idea around the biggest and most sophisticated issuers, believing they would quickly understand the validity of their idea. Their track record and contacts got them audiences pretty easily. The word around was that when they went to Chase, they were politely laughed out of the room with a consensus that it couldn't work. Imagine the reaction of cardholders when they discuss the interest rate on their credit card with friends only to find there were substantial differences. The fact that the likelihood of such a discussion actually ever taking place was negligible didn't seem to matter.

Citibank was not much smarter. I was in the meeting when Rich and Nigel made their pitch. My boss deferred to the guru of consumer credit who maintained it was just not possible to analytically discriminate among cardholders on the basis of probability of default to such a fine degree that pricing could be based on the analysis. You couldn't create reliable profit models for customer segments defined by risk. The data was just not good enough.

Rich and Nigel believed enough in their idea to keep shopping it around until they found a small bank in Maryland, Signet, which was in serious trouble, but it had a small yet viable credit card business. It was too small to sell for much, but the board believed enough in Rich and Nigel's concept to cut a deal to launch the concept in their portfolio. It worked. Soon, Capital One was born.

Not only was the strategy a great success, but Capital One, by the nature of its business model, took market share of the very best customer segments, the lowest risk yet habitual revolvers, and they did so in huge numbers. These customers borrowed with their cards and didn't default. These were the most profitable customers in the credit card business. Capital One walked into a situation where the industry was paralyzed in its inability to respond to its aggressive pricing without cannibalizing its own revenue stream. It sat back and bled market share for years until it finally created its own capability to create tiered pricing based on tiered creditworthiness.

Both Chase and Citi executives used their gut to assess the idea that Rich and Nigel presented. They fundamentally judged them to be smart guys who just didn't understand the realities of the credit card business. They saw patterns that did not apply. They didn't slow down to carefully listen to Rich and Nigel and analyze their proposal. It came back to haunt them in a major way.

There are many, many examples of instinctive decision-making gone awry. One of the more famous ones is of the prior head of FEMA, General Matthew Broderick. On August 29, 2005, in the midst of Hurricane Katrina, Broderick relied on his experiences and instincts and decided to delay initiating the FEMA's response because the reports on the ground regarding breaches of the levy were conflicting. However, he had no experience with a hurricane and a city built below sea level.

All this is not to say that experience has no value in decision-making. Quite the contrary. In a subsequent discussion on the work of Edward Tsang, we'll learn that experience substantially improves *computational intelligence*, a key component of the decision-making process discussed below. Not surprisingly, there is a great deal of distance in this capability between the novice and the experienced decision-maker.

Bounded rationality: This one is inescapable. Rationality has its limitations. The concept of bounded rationality emerged from mathematicians. Any decision that we make requires three things: information, analytical capability, and time (to gather information and analyze it). All three are limited. Expanding any of the three costs money and/or runs the risk of the decision becoming moot. Acquiescing to these conditions limits the rationality of the decision. The decision-maker then is a *satisficer* rather than an optimizer. They resort to simplification of both conditions and criteria as well as using heuristics to cope with the limitations rather than some rigid optimization model.

This is where the value of experience comes in. The experienced decision-maker will be a better satisficer than the novice. Edward Tsang argues the rationality of a decision-maker is limited by their *computational intelligence*, which is the combination of their algorithms and heuristics.

These formulas and rules of thumb are the product of both intelligence and experience. The more of each, the stronger your computational intelligence will be. That's the value of experience.

The essence of Tsang's hypothesis is that experience expands the boundaries of rationality in decision-making. The inexperienced operate in a small ring-fenced area and need much more investment of time, information gathering, and analysis than the experienced decision-maker. In big decisions, the difference can't be made up with more time and energy. The gap is too wide. That's what separates the CEO from the genius executive two or three levels down in the organization.

In support of this, Garry Kasparov, world-famed chess player, argues that we should learn how to trust our guts. Intuition is everything in chess and in life, he says. There are 10^{120} moves in chess. That's more than the number of seconds since the big bang created the universe. It's more than the number of atoms in the universe. It approximates a mathematically infinite number of moves—even though real infinity would be that to the power of infinity.

How do we find our way in this ocean of possibilities? How could Kasparov fight a machine that could make tens of millions of calculations per second? How could he successfully make the tradeoff of material (number of pieces gained or lost) versus quality (the stature of those pieces and their positions on the board). And then there's time versus material and quality? The clock is always ticking. Tick, tock, tick, tock, tick, tock.

It's all about intuition, Kasparov says. In the decision-making process, "It's 1 percent calculation or less and 99 percent of understanding and finding intuitive ways." We have many opportunities where we cannot foresee all the consequences (uncertainty). In life, we can't see all the possibilities either. We have only one choice. We have to learn to trust our intuition, our instincts, and our guts.

How do we square this with Kahneman and Tversky? Experience increases one's computational intelligence, a part of *bounded rationality*. The greater the experience, the greater the computational intelligence. This is a big part of separates the champion chess player from the intermediate chess player. So, Kasparov is fully in sync with Kahneman and Tversky.

There is not much more to be said about this source of irrationality. Books have been written about it, but for our purposes, suffice it to say: it's out there. We have to be aware of it and live with it as best we can. I think the most important learning on bounded rationality comes from the work of Tsang on the value of experience as it expands one's computational intelligence.

Multiple Biases—John Lasseter's Story

Frequently, biases from several categories weigh in to create irrational decisions. As you read through the following case, see what biases you can identify. We'll compare notes at the end of the story.

John Lasseter was an animator at Walt Disney Feature Animation, the realization of a childhood dream. Through a series of coincidences, he was exposed to the nascent computer-generated imagery and quickly identified its potential in animation. With some colleagues, he pursued a project to use the technique. Unwittingly, they got on the wrong side of their immediate superiors in doing so. The project was canceled because the perceived cost-benefit analysis was unfavorable.

Lasseter was summarily fired. He then went on to join the graphics group of the computer division of Lucasfilm, which was later sold to Steve Jobs. It went on to become Pixar. Later, Disney bought Pixar from Jobs at a valuation of $7.4 billion. Lasseter was named chief creative officer of both Pixar and Walt Disney Animation Studios, a position he still holds. He has won two Academy Awards.

Of course, we can't know what went on in the minds of the Disney executives who decided to fire Lasseter. However, if we think through the biases identified above, it is pretty clear some combination of stability bias (anchored to existing methods of animation production), instinctive decision-making (dealing with subordinate behavior that bypassed the corporate approval process), and action-oriented biases (this needs to be stopped now and cannot be tolerated) all played roles.

Smart People Do Stupid Things

There is no gardening without humility. Nature is constantly sending even its oldest scholars to the bottom of the class for some egregious blunder.
—*Alfred Austin, British poet*

One of the great things about failure is there's so much material to work with. One of my favorites is the choice of Chuck Prince as CEO of Citigroup. The story begins with Sandy Weil's (CEO of Travelers Insurance) clever engineering of a merger between Travelers and Citigroup. John Reed, a brilliant individual, had been CEO of Citigroup prior to the merger. Sandy and John became co-CEOs. It's always only a question of time before the structure like this disintegrates.

Sandy made his mark on Citigroup remarkably quickly. First, as a street-smart guy, he won the CEO position of Citigroup in a management shake-up. Once again, street smarts overcame brilliance in the rough-and-tumble world of business. Second, and perhaps more important, he transitioned the culture of Citigroup from highly decentralized to tribal. He was the chief. Third, and probably most deadly, he named Chuck Prince as his successor.

Chuck was an attorney who had been Sandy's "deals guy." He had never led or managed much of anything prior to finding himself on the throne of Citigroup. He had zero experience with regulated companies.

He was not a banker! And here he was the CEO of the largest bank in the world. What were Sandy and the board thinking? Sandy had clearly mesmerized the board.

It was 2003. He went on to become chairman of the board in 2006. He also proceeded to almost destroy Citigroup by taking an outsized mortgage-related risk. In July 2007, Chuck said, "As long as the music keeps playing, you got to get up and dance. We (Citigroup) are still dancing." Talk about herd psychology. Talk about smart people doing dumb things. Wow!

Citigroup was tied for first with Bank of America in terms of banks taking the largest amount ($45 billion) of government bailout (TARP) money. This must be the pinnacle of crowd thinking going stupid and smart people going along for the ride. More on the wisdom of crowds follows.

Are the Many Smarter Than the Few?

Sometimes even a smart crowd will make a mistake.
—James Surowiecki

Notwithstanding the opening quote, Surowiecki's hypothesis on crowd thinking has a lot going for it. Aggregating input from many people is frequently a robust process for reaching decisions. In fact, I would argue the free market is brilliant at setting price and allocating resources—most of the time. But it also can be disastrously wrong, just as the quote implies. Myriad asset bubbles throughout history are evidence of this.

One would expect the rational man to be at his finest on Wall Street where the combined analytical genius of the best financial minds in the world have much of the global economy in their collective hands. However, people are irrational. Markets are made up of people. Therefore, markets can be—and all too often are—irrational. On the one hand, they are the best mechanism known to man to establish price; conversely, they can be at times, very, very wrong in appropriately reflecting value.

Once revered as the finest central banker of all time, Alan Greenspan relied heavily on that rationality as he pressed for more deregulation than had taken place in a hundred years. He reversed the tide that ensued following the Great Depression.

His thesis, born in a lifelong commitment to Libertarianism (the advocacy of a government funded voluntarily and limited to protecting individuals from coercion and violence), bankers would act within the bounds of reason to control the risk run by their institutions to a level that would ensure the preservation of their respective institutions without government interference.

What Greenspan overlooked was that banks are governed by herd psychology when earnings are under pressure. They all reach for higher risk investments to improve the yield (earnings) on their assets. They often take on more debt (increased leverage means increased risk) to buy these assets.

The greater the pressure on earnings, the more these tendencies occur. Systemically, these are self-defeating and dangerous as they create bubbles (asset classes that become overpriced due to heavy demand). The *risk premium* they should offer the market becomes mispriced, and the risk/reward equation becomes distorted.

I was a part of this happening with the Latin American debt crisis in the seventies and eighties. I have clear recollections of a senior executive visiting Mexico in the late seventies and rebuking local management for losing market share in cross-border dollar lending to both the public and private sectors. I also remember well a very senior executive making a farewell visit to Brazil upon retirement. He was given a parting gift: a primitive painting by a famous local artist depicting him running across the Brazilian countryside tossing dollar bills everywhere to smiling locals. I sometimes wonder where that painting hangs today.

They were both part of an over exuberant market in the midst of herd psychology that reckoned a good way to recycle petrodollars was to lend them to less developed countries (they were called less developed countries (LDCs) before they became emerging markets). This brilliant solution came to an abrupt end when Mexico raised its hand and said it could no longer pay its debt. Brazil was next, and others fell like dominoes. It was a classic bubble.

The combined losses to the banking system relative to their capital levels was greater than it was in the 2008/09 global financial crisis.

It had less global economic impact because the credit markets did not freeze up like they did in the fourth quarter of 2008 and the first quarter of 2009. Since balance sheets and respective exposures were more transparent than in'08/'09, assessing counterparty risk was easier.

In the subprime mortgage debacle, the same phenomenon occurred. The market was awash in liquidity seeking higher yielding assets in the face of historically low interest rates for benchmark American government debt instruments. A flattening yield curve was putting banks under earnings pressure because interest rate gapping profits (funding long-term assets with short-term liabilities at much lower interest rates) melted away.

Try as he did, Alan Greenspan was unable to push long-dated treasury bonds' interest rates up along with the increases he was driving in short-term rates from 2005 through 2007. All he did was exacerbate the problem by squeezing gapping profits.

Banks responded, as they invariably do, by reaching for more risk. They did this by increasing leverage (borrowing more money to buy more assets), which added financial risk to their business, by engaging in the subprime business fraught with dangerous assumptions and by participating in off-balance sheet activities to generate profits while masking (legally) their exposure.

And then there was the *shadow banking system*, which was essentially unregulated banking. Each of these brought more systemic risk that was only fully understood in hindsight. Nobody added up the numbers except for a negligible number of players in a system involving thousands of players globally.

Also, people and markets are overly influenced by the past. Warren Buffett said, "In the business world, the rearview mirror is always clearer than the windshield." Of course, the rational thing to do is to look to the future. If we look at the irrationality of markets for equities after the Great Depression, it was the 1950s before there was a return to normalcy.

The same happened with start-ups and IPOs building to the dot-com bubble and the years that followed. The risk of start-ups got pushed higher and higher up the food chain to where venture capitalists took on the risk of angel investors and IPOs were done so early their risk characteristics were more like the risk VC's rationally take in normal markets. The market for IPOs and VC money is still in recovery some twelve years later.

Marc Andreessen was interviewed in the *Harvard Business Review* in May 2013:

> HBR: Are you saying that the general view of the market is irrational?

> Andreessen: Yeah, it's irrational. The natural thing is to focus on the future, not the past. But current attitudes are very much based on what happened in the past.

This is the recency bias, which is expecting the experiences of the past six months to continue for the next six months and longer.

If we take a step back and consider how we make decisions, irrationality is perhaps more the norm than the aberration. It is certainly commonplace and often found where we would least expect it. Perhaps Friedrich Nietzsche had a point when he wrote, "How did reason come into the world? As is fitting, in an irrational manner, by accident."

Minimizing Irrationality

Wouldn't economics make a lot more sense if it were based on how people actually behave, instead of how they should behave?
—Dan Ariely[4]

I would be surprised if the stories and the analysis above do not cause you to recognize irrationality in some of your own experiences. Irrationality is an omnipresent problem. Our emotions can be controlled, but they cannot be eliminated. We are by our nature emotional creatures and thus bring various biases to the table.

Fortunately, there are many things we can do to limit its deleterious impact on decision-making. The obvious first thing is awareness. We need to step away from the impressions that are created by our environment and education that teach us that decision-makers are rational when they are not. More specifically, we need to embrace the

4. *Predictably Irrational: The Hidden Forces That Shape Our Decisions*, Daniel Ariely.

thought that it's really difficult to be rational. Only then can we begin to cope and effectively manage this dilemma.

Kahneman, Lovallo, and Sibony argue we cannot eliminate our personal biases because they arise from our instinctive thought processes, which include our visual and associative memory. These instinctive thought processes form our interpretations of what is going on around us and are subject to context. They also include things like our past experiences, emotions, and goals. Kahneman argues these instinctive processes are "fast" and cannot be eliminated. They are distinctly different from our reflective thought processes that are "slow, effortful, and deliberate."

While we may not be able to eliminate our personal biases or even recognize which ones we might have, if we can embrace the concept that they exist and that they get us into trouble in decision-making, we can invest the time and energy to minimize their impact. What follows are some key steps we can take to accomplish that.

Process, Process, Process: Generally speaking, decision-making has five major elements: definition of the matter to be decided; fact gathering; analysis; a process to vet the analysis; and judgment of the decision-maker or -makers. These elements are often depicted as a waterfall connoting linearity, but that is not the way it happens.

In sound decision-making, the five elements involve multiple ad hoc feedback loops. As just one example, the vetting of analysis process often leads to more information gathering and/or revised analysis. Also, the vetting process should be applied to the judgment of decision-makers before the choice is finalized.

Not surprisingly, each of the five needs to be strong for good decisions to be made. What is surprising is Lovalo and Sibony's research found that strong process was the single most important of the five by far.

In reviewing more than one thousand decisions ranging from product launches to capital expenditures to acquisitions, they found "process mattered more than analysis—by a factor of six." This conclusion can be extended to problem definition and fact gathering. Good process ferrets out weaknesses in all three. My experience would say that process is most important in vetting the judgment of decision-makers as well.

Consider the credit card portfolio acquisition story. The decision outcome may have been entirely different if the decision-making process included a loop back to folks not in the room to vet their reactions to the choice being made by the decision-maker. The analysis in the binder I carried into the room was not even discussed, though it had been reviewed by all present. It clearly didn't underpin the decision on the bid. And even the binder, as rational as it purported to be, was fraught with biases.

As I mentioned earlier, the credit, marketing, treasury, and operations departments that provided the key inputs to our model were biased. We all suffered from Jack Welch's deal heat.

My bid was already over the top. And that's not just Monday-morning quarterbacking. Beyond the fact that the binder was full of its own biases, John didn't benefit from an open and frank discussion of it. Our process broke down in the final stage. It was my job as CFO to ensure such a breakdown didn't happen. Conflict of interest bias was at play: my self-interests (my career, fear of reprisal) versus the corporation's interest. So, the resulting failure was in part on my doorstep. I was an ineffective decision influencer.

Less obvious perhaps but nonetheless pertinent is the Colombian story I told in chapter 1. I think a sound vetting process would have uncovered the vulnerability of my single-way-out strategy with no plan B. It may also have questioned our underlying assumption that we were in a dangerous position with the existing shareholders in the first place given the track record of a trouble-free relationship. Combine this with the vagaries of acquisitions and the unique nature of the parties (the Catholic Church as an investor and business partner and a dissident set of Colombian shareholders as sellers), and what were the odds of success? How could one rationally lead senior management into thinking this was a done deal before the documents were inked? I will return to process and its importance in my later discussion on complexity.

One of the key aspects of process involves the people around us and how we engage them. What follows is a compendium of critical skills, conditions, and methodologies, which when combined, will help increase the rationality in your decisions. It won't bulletproof it. That's not possible to do because—unless you've relegated your decision-making process to a computer—there will always be human beings involved, as well there should be. And human beings are emotional creatures. We've already discussed at length what that means.

The bottom line on process is that deciding how to decide is often more important than the decision itself.

Skills: The single most important skill that you as a decision-maker must develop to successfully contain the risks inherent in irrationality is the ability to listen. It's the single most highly underrated communications skill. We confuse hearing with listening and often lose all sense in a discussion of the speaker's point of view, particularly if there is disagreement involved.

Using emotional terms like "that's not true" or "that's wrong" versus "I don't see it that way" or simply "I disagree" cause us to click off and stop listening. Also, once it's clear to us that the speaker disagrees with our point of view, we start thinking about our counterpoints. Almost everyone overestimates his or her listening skills.

Many years ago, I had the privilege of working with a consultant named Doug Smith.[5] Ex-McKinsey, Doug was working solo at the time and we Bank had him under retainer at American Express. By that time, he had authored one of the best business books that has ever been written on teams. It has sold over one million copies.

Doug was the adviser of a team effort that I will describe later in this chapter. Doug taught me a trick to determine if you have listened. If you can explain, in your own words, the other person's point of view to their satisfaction, then you have listened. You don't have to agree with their point of view—just demonstrate that you understand it. Try it. You'll be surprised how infrequently you can do it for some combination of the reasons I mentioned above. Of course, it's fair game to ask the other person in the discussion to do the same. Since you know the trick and they don't, the odds that they can do it is substantially lower. Doing this is not as easy as it sounds. It takes work. It takes practice. But the effort is worthwhile. This skill is important in

---

5. *The Wisdom of Teams,* Douglas K. Smith and Jon R. Katzenbach, HarperCollins.

many things. In de-biasing your decision-making, it's critical.

Culture: A key condition for rational decision-making is a culture where candid feedback is encouraged. It needs to promote dissenting opinions, and it should do this without regard to hierarchy. Everybody's view should be heard. Here is an example of such an environment.

Mohamed El Erian was chief executive officer and co-chief investment officer of PIMCO at the time that this story took place. Shortly after he joined the firm from his position as the deputy director of the International Monetary Fund, he was in a staff meeting. As he finished expressing a point of view on an issue, a young intern spoke up with an opposing view. In the ensuing discussion, both views were considered on their relative merits without regard to the source. As Mohamed tells the story, he then knew he had joined the right firm.

If you are not operating in this sort of environment, you will need to seek out people to include in your decision-making process who are both knowledgeable and candid—people who will give you their unvarnished point of view. Include people from other areas who have no skin in the game. An example of this was shared by Mary Meeker, an executive at the prestigious venture capital firm Kleiner, Perkins, and she is sometimes referred to as the "queen of the internet." As Mary tells it, partners in the firm take ownership of the investments they bring to the firm. However, another partner who has limited skin in the game is assigned to live the customer experience of the investment and give feedback to the investment committee on what that experience is like. This becomes an important part of the firm's evaluation of their investments. It's a great way to contain champion bias and confirmation bias.

Mentors: The word *mentor* originated with the character Mentor in Homer's *Odyssey*. The goddess Athena, acting through Mentor, provides advice to Odysseus's son while Odysseus is away in the Trojan War. Today, mentorship is generally thought of as a great way to guide and promote someone's career. In fact, firms like McKinsey have formal mentorship programs.

I believe a mentor is someone whose brain you can pick, who will listen hard to your problems and opportunities, and who has the knowledge and wisdom to nudge you in the right direction. Mentors at all levels in the organization can be invaluable. Of the Fortune 500 CEOs surveyed, 75 percent mentioned mentors as one of the top three factors that enabled their success. A good mentor is a sounding board that should bring a different and dispassionate perspective to a decision. In this regard, it's a good idea to think of your mentors as a "personal board of directors." Sure, they can be used for career guidance, but their other value is in broader decision-making.

In forming your board, consider the expertise of candidates for board seats. Don't only look for the wisdom of elders, though the best mentors are often older than you. Seek out people with expertise you lack. Round out your personal board with skills that complement each of the members. Mentors should not have a direct relationship with you, either reporting lines in the organization or personal relationship. There should be no fear of repercussions to stymie candid feedback.

The mentor-mentee relationship must be a close bond to be useful. It must be nurtured as it takes time to develop. The mentor must be willing to give, and the mentee must be willing to receive. A mentor must have the energy and courage to be candid and honest without being hurtful. Trust, confidence, and responsibility are integral parts of the relationship. This all goes in both directions—mentor to mentee and vice versa.

Developing your personal board will take time and effort to accomplish, but you'll find it to be well worth it. The process itself has value, and the development is ongoing. It's also a two-way street. While the principle reward for a good mentor is giving, it will also be appropriate for the mentee to give back. Passing on an article that you stumbled upon that falls in the wheelhouse of a mentor, an occasional update phone call where there is no request for assistance, or an invitation to lunch where you insist on paying are just a few of the ways that a mentee can express their appreciation of the contribution made by the mentor.

Choose your mentors wisely because they can do harm as well as good. They may give instinctive advice. We already discussed the dangers of that. You'll have to employ the same tests to their advice as you apply when you encounter your own instinctive decisions. These are described in a later section of this chapter. You'll need to consider their biases, but that will be easier to do than to account for your own. Yours are hard for you to spot. Theirs will be, relatively speaking, much easier for you to spot (though not for them). Also, they have an important advantage; they have little or no skin in the game (except their relationship with you of course) if you choose them correctly.

Diversity: In an organization, diversity is critically important. It can be brought to the organization in various ways. The first thing executives can do is to hire people that are different from them. It is the first line of defense against the social biases of sunflower management and groupthink.

Diversity comes in various forms. Gender, race, sexual orientation, creed, ethnic background, business background, and age are the most prevalent bases for discrimination. Let me address the last one first, but perhaps in a way you will not expect. When Jack Welch decided the venerable GE should actively engage in e-commerce, he hired someone in his thirties who had significant experience in the field. And, when that guy talked, Welch listened. He also encouraged his subordinates to do the same.

Differing perspectives have immense value when tackling complex problems, and strategic issues are most always complex (the subject of the next chapter). The value of talking through the problem with a diverse set of participants is the process develops a richer sense of context, and solutions often emerge from the process itself not on the table at the outset.

Strong subordinates: An executive's accomplishments are delivered by subordinates. The smartest thing you can do to get ahead is to hire people who are top 10 percent performers and are capable of replacing you. Besides, having your team chomping at your heels will keep you on your toes. I think the single most important thing we can do to minimize the impact of irrationality in our decision-making is to surround ourselves with the smartest, most competent, and most outspoken people we can. Never be afraid to hire somebody who you think is smarter than you.

Further, and just as importantly, they should be different from you in their views, approaches, and interests. The worst thing we can do is to surround ourselves with people who think like we do. There's little value added, and it is also fraught with danger of groupthink or managing up. Being reluctant to hire people smarter than you is a big mistake.

First, your success is largely determined by the work of the people you manage. Their competency or lack thereof reflects in a direct way on you. In some respects, you are the people you choose. Choose those who will make a positive difference and those who will, from time to time, save you from yourself.

I had a personal experience along these lines when I became a CFO at Citibank. While I knew finance pretty well, I had not taken anything other than basic accounting. I always made sure that I hired the smartest accounting policy person I could find, all the better if they were smarter than me. When I became the CFO of Citibank's credit card group, I hired John Gerspach as my accounting policy person. John is the current CFO of Citigroup, the entire corporation.

The premortem: The premortem was made popular by Gary Klein. It applies *prospective hindsight* or Saturday- (rather than Monday-) morning quarterbacking to a project, but it works equally well with a decision prior to implementation.

To do one, the decision-maker brings together the key players and says something like, "Imagine the results are in, and this decision has been a major failure. I want each of you to write down the reasons why. We'll then go around the room and discuss each item, one at a time." The leader must press for an open and candid discussion in order for the exercise to have value. Nobody gets off the hook. Everybody must participate.

The premortem is a great way to bring out risks and might show ways to mitigate those risks. In the extreme, it may change the decision itself. In any event, it is always valuable to conduct one. Bear in mind that the value of the premortem will directly relate to the culture of the firm, the strength and diversity of the subordinates/participants, and how good a listener you are.

Harnessing instinctive decision-making: We've already discussed the dangers of instinctive decision-making. However, under certain conditions, it can be useful. As importantly, the influence of our instincts can't be avoided as Campbell and Whitehead point out. Their inherent biases influence many things in decision-making from where we seek information and where we don't, whom we listen to and whom we don't, how we choose to frame the problem in the first place, and when we decide we have reached the boundaries of the value/risks of continuing to spend more time and money gathering data and analyzing it. They provide tests we can use to help us feel confident that we are drawing on appropriate experiences and emotions, i.e., our biases are limited.

These four tests include:

1. The familiarity test: This means searching our memories for identical or at least similar experiences to the one being addressed. As already discussed, the foundation for instinctive decision-making is pattern recognition. I previously put forth the caveat that in strategic decisions, patterns are not often similar. In my view (and Daniel Kahneman's), this test isn't easy to pass, particularly in the types of decisions I'm discussing because we're not talking about crisis situations where time is highly compressed to hours, minutes, or seconds. Generally speaking, we don't give this test sufficient dispassionate scrutiny before we deem it passed. I encourage caution here.

2. The feedback test: We all tend to remember our decisions as sound. But were they? Certainly, if we're going to apply the patterns to the present decision, they have to be. Were your previous decisions that fit this pattern perceived to be the right decision by others? Why? Was the feedback candid and analytically sound? Was there a credible postmortem that included representatives of all involved as well as your mentors? I find this to be the most important test of all because it's the one where you have the opportunity to uncover your personal biases including the two mentioned below.

3. The measured-emotions test: We must ensure emotionally charged experiences are separated from the current decision. These experiences color our thinking on similar situations and thus may bias us. This test needs to be closely linked with the feedback test above because that's the best way to identify

whether our emotions were measured.

4. The independence test: Are you being influenced by any inappropriate personal interests or attachments that may compromise your rationality? Again, this test needs to be closely linked with the feedback test because that's the best way to ferret out such influences.

The criteria are sound, but strong process must be applied to ensure you meet them. The feedback test is central to that process.

Doin' It Right—A Case Study

When I was president of American Express Bank, it became clear the bank's operating system needed to be replaced. Our decades-old legacy system was a Rube Goldberg kluge of more than 2 million lines of spaghetti code, much of which were undocumented. It was an accident waiting to happen. Steve Goldstein, the CEO, and I were skeptical about our in-house competency in the systems' area.

Not long after they had embarked on the effort, it was clear that user involvement in creating the requirements for the system had atrophied. In a highly dangerous combination of frustration and arrogance, the systems team decided they knew enough about the bank's needs to go forward with virtually no user involvement. Anybody who knows systems development knows that is the road to perdition."

Steve and I felt we needed to consider a radically different approach and embarked on a process to decide whether to outsource the effort. This was radical thinking in the bank and in the corporation, but we mustered support to expend the resources to conduct a study and make a yay-or-nay decision. Yay would mean a ten-year outsourcing contract valued at about $300 million, which, in 1994, was a considerable sum. It would also mean about 250 of our employees would become employees of the contract winner. Fear of the devil you don't know made this a troublesome proposition for most concerned.

If we were going to do it, it had to both the right decision and one supported by the organization. If the process resulted in a nay, it would show us where our weaknesses were and give us an opportunity to strengthen them.

We formed the "One-Bank Partnership Team" of the executive committee: two of my direct reports and me. The name was meant to deliver the message to all employees of the bank that the mission of this effort was to unite historically disparate branches and businesses spread over thirty-five countries. Our team would cause them to act as one bank.

Doug Smith was an adviser to the team. He set the ground rules. They included: at team meetings, everyone at the table spoke with an equal voice (rank did not have its privileges); everyone had to do real work on the team effort in between meetings, work should be roughly equally distributed; we had to listen to each other's point of view; and a major part of our work would be communicating with the organization what we were doing and deciding with an emphasis on why so that the bank's middle management and staff were kept informed. We hired First Manhattan Consulting, which had a dedicated portion of its practice to outsourcing systems decisions to help us develop a request for proposal (RFP).

We developed a briefing manual that each team member had and used to keep our subordinates and their teams up to date on what we were doing and what we were thinking. We solicited feedback. We held town hall meetings. We got significant feedback. Some of it was not positive, particularly from the systems' organization that would be outsourced if we went that route. We literally traveled around the world in this effort. It was that important. In the end, it came down to three choices: EDS (Electronic Data Systems, Ross Perot's old company); Accenture; or keeping the project in-house. It was an effort that lasted about nine months.

The Accenture people were about the smartest I've ever worked with. They provided us a brilliant two-word descriptor of a winning strategy for us. Our space in the market was as a *nimble follower*. Brilliant. Being stuck in the middle was deadly and accounted of the bank's historically weak performance. Given our small size, we certainly couldn't afford to lead.

EDS said if the development effort ever got into trouble with our employees under their management, they would "darken the sky with eagles." In other words, they would send in the marines. Brilliant.

The One-Bank Partnership Team vote was unanimous. We went with EDS. We needed the marines. This was, without a doubt, the best business decision I've ever had the privilege to be a part of. The One-Bank Partnership Team decided to outsource all systems' development and data centers in a ten-year, $300 million contract. In 1994, that was real money, particularly for a bank with $16 billion in total assets.

There are some critical lessons to take away from this story. First, note the process of inclusion. Second, note the involvement of disinterested parties with appropriate expertise. Third, note the massive effort in communications throughout the organization. The result of the disciplined, inclusive process was organization consensus, no surprises, and a satisficing outcome. In the words of Daft Punk, everybody was "dancin' 'cause we were doin' it right." Deciding how to decide was key.

CHAPTER 3
COMPLEXITY: DON'T FIGHT IT~EMBRACE IT

Life Is Messy

Life is really simple, but we insist on making it complicated.

—Confucius

My perspective differs from Confucius. In fact, I believe we insist on oversimplifying our approaches to inherently complex situations. That increases our probability of failure. Complexity must be embraced—not resisted. But before it can be embraced, much like failure itself, it must be understood.

About a dozen years ago, I spent a year in the woods of Vermont studying complexity science and chaos theory. It wasn't like Walden Pond, but it was close. My dog never forgave me because it was just the two of us; being an extrovert, I pestered her endlessly.

I was working with a team of business consultants, including a couple of experts on the subject. One of them, Mary Ann Allison, had even written a book on it. Our mission was to create a consulting business focused on helping companies apply the concepts of complexity science to organizational design and behavior. The underlying concept was that complexity science provides insights in business situations that could help optimize performance, particularly with innovation. In fact, I'm convinced to this day that it does. That's what this chapter is about, at least in part. Nonetheless, this story doesn't have a happy ending.

We worked virtually from widespread locations with a nexus in New York City where we held face-to-face meetings every month or two. I lived in Vermont because I had a vacation home there. It was an opportunity to live in a beautiful but isolated place with many fond memories. We worked well together and were a driven team. We hammered out what we felt was a sound approach to conducting an engagement and how we would pitch our services to corporate executives.

Through our many contacts, we had pretty good access to C-suite decision-makers. We began to make our pitches. However, despite our preparation and efforts, we kept striking out. People listened (or seemed to), but they would not commit to an engagement.

Along the way, we often spoke about why we were failing. Our hypothesis was that our prospects were not yet intellectually or emotionally ready for our proposals. Also, our underlying concepts were too difficult to explain and for them to conceptualize. We would get caught up in the vocabulary of this arcane science, reaching for metaphors like the weather, the behavior of ant colonies and swarming bees. The weather is a nonlinear system as demonstrated by the butterfly effect. A butterfly flapping its wings in Brazil can create a hurricane off the coast of Miami. Small variations in input can cause large changes in output. Ant colonies and bees demonstrate the concept of self-organization.

Our point was that the same would be true of organizations during periods of change, provided there is a strong culture (values and behavioral norms) to guide behavior in chaos. All that was required was to give up command and control, establish context, and allow your organization to self-organize. We used these metaphors to describe how innovation comes from allowing an organization to move to the edge of chaos. "Order will emerge. Trust us. After all, it has for ants and bees."

We were a start-up, and our proposed approach lacked credibility. The research behind our hypotheses was fundamentally a collection of anecdotal evidence and metaphors that were unconvincing to everyone but us. Or perhaps it was that our potential clients lacked confidence in the strength of their culture to guide actions of independent agents through periods of chaos. No matter. The deck was stacked against us. Finally, we folded our tent and went on to greener pastures. In hindsight, given the prevalence of design thinking and innovation processes in business and elsewhere, we were just ahead of our time by a decade or two.

One of our problems was that, while we had studied complexity science as a team—and understood how it applied to organizations—we did not understand it well enough to explain it to someone else. It was sort of like a student who understands a subject well enough to pass an exam. They are writing their explanations for the professor who taught them.

However, try asking them to explain the subject to one of their friends. Do they understand it well enough to teach it? Not likely. To get somebody to really understand something, you have to *overstand* it yourself. That was part of our problem. We did not overstand our ideology and couldn't teach it or sell it to skeptical senior executives. The following is my attempt to help you to understand my thesis so that you overstand it. By doing so, you can apply it and thus reduce your chances of failure.

Defining Complexity

Everything should be made as simple as possible, but not too simple.
—Albert Einstein

Our core terminology for the concept of *complexity* may be somewhat confusing. Part of that is the subject matter, and part of it is colloquially. We tend to use three of my keywords interchangeably: *complicated, complex,* and *complexity.* These words have distinct and different definitions in my lexicon.

Stepping back, my vernacular is built around descriptions of the situations we face when decisions are required, the change we want to make happen in that situation (from its current state to some desired state), and the problems we face. From this is derived an approach to solve that problem and our strategy to make that change happen. First, we'll start with situations. What's the nature of complexity in varying situations?

I define the level of complexity of situations in decision-making using four terms: *simple, complicated, complex,* and *chaotic.* I use the term complexity to describe the state of the situation. Unfortunately, this is somewhat duplicative of my using complex as one of the states. This stems from the analogies I've drawn from complexity science and complex adaptive systems for the complexity concept. This is the most straightforward way I could come up with to handle the definitions.

The concept is illustrated in diagram 1 below. Note how the shading in diagram 1 darkens and the complexity increases as we move from left to right. The gray lines are meant to indicate how, at some point, the nature of the complexity changes: first from simple to complicated, then from complicated to complex, and finally from complex to chaotic. This increase in complexity is driven by some combination of an increase in numbers of players in the situation and in the degree of freedom of action of the players.

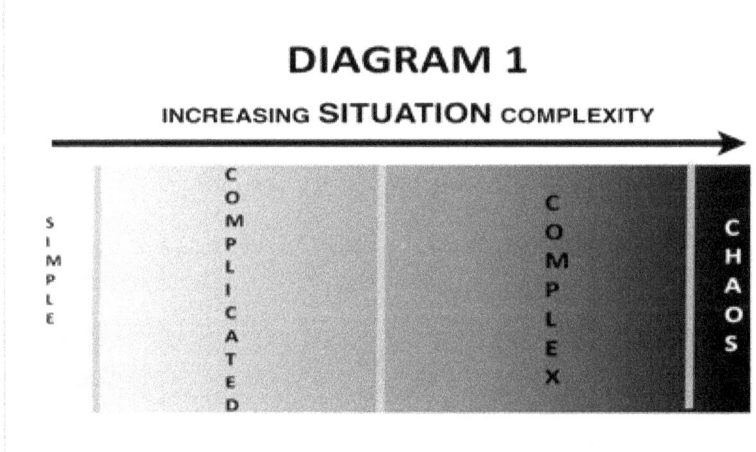

DIAGRAM 1

INCREASING SITUATION COMPLEXITY

Simple is part of this concept as the outer extreme. There are few players in these situations, and those few players have little freedom of action. All our analytical training applies in our efforts to understand these situations. Comprehension is straightforward—and so is agreement among the stakeholders on both the nature of the problem and the solution. When decisions fail in simple situations, generally they don't fail from the complexity portion of my thesis. They typically fail from irrationality.

A key aspect of simple and complicated situations is the players in the situation have limited freedom of action. The number of parts determines the level of complexity in these types of situations.

A shift supervisor in a factory is a good example of a simple situation. Let's say she/he is responsible for twenty-five employees. Each person has their assigned job. If somebody gets sick, then one of the others will backfill for her/him. Degrees of freedom are limited. Therefore, this is a pretty simple organization to manage. Performance challenges tend to be incremental, not breakthrough. Innovation isn't generally demanded. The situation is predictable. Cause-and-effect relationships are clear. With very few parts, this situation is at the simple end of the complexity spectrum.

Moving over to the right on the scale of complexity, we enter the realm of complicated situations. Compared to simple situations, complicated situations have more players. The greater the number of players, the greater the level of complexity. However, the degree of freedom of the players remains highly limited so the situation remains complicated (linear) and not complex (nonlinear).

Complicated can range from easy to understand (running a small business for example) to very, very complicated like running Foxconn, the manufacturer of the iPhone and other electronic devices. Foxconn has one million employees. That's pretty complicated.

However, it's one million people who know precisely what they're going to do when they arrive at work. Foxconn management wants it that way. They insist on it. In terms of the task at hand, they fundamentally want compliance with their instructions because they know how to best assemble the devices they have been contracted by Apple and others to construct.

Everyone in the organization has direct orders from above. Their behavioral norms and/or values define their constraints fairly tightly. They don't come to work daily with much freedom of action. And their management, right up to the top of the organization, knows what the employees are going to do each day. Their job descriptions are crystal clear. There is little to no ambiguity. Everything it takes to successfully run Foxconn is either known or knowable.

The Foxconn situation is also predictable. Its complexity is high because there are so many players. However, it's a complicated situation—not a complex one. Since we are generally dealing with human beings in our decision-making, the constraint on freedom of action is an approximation as is the resultant predictability. As long as that approximation is pretty close to reality, the situation will behave as a complicated one.

With limited degrees of freedom, complicated situations can reach even higher levels of complexity. Kennedy's decision to send a man to the moon set off a highly complicated challenge for NASA. It was complicated but not complex because what it took to succeed was either known or knowable. It was largely a matter of science and engineering—not of design or artistry. It was a matter of time and money.

Traditional analytical and problem-solving techniques worked well. Program managers, scientists, mathematicians, engineers, and others from the scientific and management arenas worked together to make it all happen. The situation exhibited clear cause-and-effect relationships. When something went wrong, with enough analysis, the cause could be determined. When something went right, the same was true. Learning from both failure and success was a relatively straightforward process. Like pieces of an intricate jigsaw puzzle, things fit together neatly. There were no mysteries like the ones that creep into the situation when the constraint on freedom of action is loosened.

One can also glean insights into complicated situations through analogies with scientific experiments. Outcomes are replicable in complicated situations. If you repeat some step, you will get the same result. Again, the processes in complicated situations are predictable. There are clear cause-and-effect relationships in complicated situations. Complicated situations have the same characteristics as simple situations; they just have more parts and higher complexity.

Taking the overstanding process one step farther, what follows is an application of the complicated situation concept to hierarchical organization structures. First, these structures were invented by the military and then institutionalized by the Catholic Church. They are a construct derived from an invention, not a discovery. They are not some natural state of affairs. They are like a smartphone and not a tree. They were created before the Industrial Revolution to get work done efficiently. They worked well in business for a century but began to crumble in their usefulness as we approached the new millennium.

The Industrial Revolution would likely still be in its early stages without this invention. Its effectiveness was built around some key assumptions. First, the people at the top of the organization understood their product, their markets, and the best processes to produce their product and satisfy their customers. Secondly, because of this knowledge, the top of the pyramid required compliance with its instructions. Information flowed in one direction: from the top down. Third, the organization's effectiveness and efficiency increased with tighter job descriptions, clearer reporting lines, and tighter controls.

The organization was rigid, and change took place slowly. It wasn't needed. It likely would have been disruptive to the well-oiled machine that was the assembly line producing a well-defined product. Also, markets evolved. They were far less frequently disrupted than they are today.

Of course, organizations don't work precisely like this. Organizations are made up of people—not machines—but the goal of all successful managers is to make their organizations operate like well-oiled machines. Henry Ford started an industry with this organizational model. Sometimes, however, the rigidity of the organization and its mental model has caused major problems. Henry Ford famously said, "People can have any color car they want as long as it's black." That enabled the birth of General Motors. With its multicolor product offerings, it grew larger than Ford and never looked back—until the Japanese manufacturers blindsided them and disrupted the industry.

Decades later, this same arrogant mind-set of dictating to customers what they wanted in a car and believing they (Detroit) knew everything there was to know about quality in auto production provided Japanese manufacturers the opportunity to enter the American market and eventually dominate it. Toyota relegated General Motors to a weak second place in the global car market by focusing on the customer with a superior-quality product. It figured out how to make a high-quality product at an attractive price, and GM couldn't compete.

There is a story about GM purchasing a Toyota and reverse engineering the engine. They were mystified as to how an engine of that quality could be made at the price. In the global financial crisis, global car sales plummeted. GM was so weakened it needed a government bailout to keep it from liquidation.

From the Complicated to the Complex

> For want of a nail, the shoe was lost;
> For want of a shoe, the horse was lost;
> For want of a horse, the rider was lost;
> For want of a rider, the battle was lost;
> For want of a battle, the kingdom was lost;
> And all for want of a horseshoe nail.
>
> —Anonymous

As we move across the spectrum in diagram 1 from complicated to complex, it is both numbers of parts and the freedom of action of those parts that determine the level of complexity of a situation. As the constraints on the freedom of action of the parts in a situation are loosened, the nature of complexity changes from complicated to complex.

Most all the situations we deal with and make decisions about involve people. People, of course, by their very nature, have freedom of action and interaction. The only reason so many situations can successfully be treated as complicated is because the freedom of action of the people involved is limited by various constraints (job descriptions, direction from superiors, culture, etc.). The marginally complex situation can be treated as complicated. The approximation works.

That shift manager example was a simple situation because it had few parts with limited degrees of freedom. But let's suppose there is a sudden spurt of growth in production required. The shift manager is faced with a challenge that likely jumps into the complex arena.

Not only does the level of complexity increase because the number of parts likely increases to include more workers, but it also changes in nature. It's likely the shift manager will need to team up with his subordinates to solve the opaque problem of how best to respond to the challenge. You can no longer meaningfully assess the situation by analyzing the shift manager and her subordinates. You need to analyze how they interact and the ramifications of that interaction. The operation becomes messy at least until a solution is found.

All bets are off on the normal functioning of that shift manager's operation. It's predictability plummets. Perhaps its performance does as well. Cause-and-effect relationships will become clouded rather than clear. Problems can no longer be parsed. The situation must be considered a whole. Worse still, if we apply classic management tools, they can lead to false assumptions, rigid strategies, and—almost invariably—failed decisions.

Many important things in the situation will no longer be replicable. Predictability is gone. Also, all parties need to be very cautious about instinctive decision-making since there are few clear historical patterns to draw upon. The criteria for successful instinctive decision-making discussed in chapter 2 are not met. And it's not just insufficient patterns. There would be no credible historical feedback.

Going back to Foxconn, a tragedy befell the company that led to a public relations nightmare. In 2010, eighteen employees attempted suicide resulting in fourteen deaths. In reaction to the incidents, Apple and HP, two of its largest customers, pressed Foxconn to improve working conditions. This was in spite of the fact that the suicide rate of Foxconn employees was lower than that in China and each of the fifty states in the United States. Nonetheless, running Foxconn went from complicated (status quo) to complex/chaotic (crisis management) virtually overnight.

After the crisis was over, it was back to business as usual. However, it returned to a complicated situation quickly because that's what Foxconn is all about: many players with a lack of freedom of action. You can run a quality-focused, efficient manufacturing operation with a relatively rigid environment. Management knows the customer requirements because Apple writes them down. Foxconn management wants *compliance*—not creativity. That means employees have limited degrees of freedom, and the approximation of a complicated situation works.

Complex situations give us the opportunity to be in command without control. This is not for the faint of heart. But if we're sufficiently adaptive in our decision-making and if we can get ourselves comfortable with trial and error, patterns will emerge in the situation over time. We need to adapt our mental models to become stronger in a Darwinian sense. But there's nothing positive about chaos, the last classification in our model. It is a state where patterns are not discernible. They are unknowable. Further, interrelationships are not understandable.

The overstanding process needs to be approached from various perspectives. More examples will help. Here is how I first experienced varying levels of complexity.

I grew up in a town of about two thousand Polish, Catholic onion farmers and I was one of them. My father was the oldest of nine brothers and one sister. My grandfather forced him to quit grammar school two months before graduation because he was needed on the onion farm. He was never allowed to go back. He didn't have choices. He became an onion farmer and drove a truck in a lumberyard. He also disproved the old "saw" that hard work never killed anybody. He had his first heart attack at fifty and died at sixty-nine.

My mother, my two sisters, and I worked the onion fields, first as sharecroppers and later, when my parents had accumulated enough savings, as landowners. My mother worked in a department store to make ends meet. Life was simple, relatively speaking.

I have fond memories of those simpler days. One of my sisters, Roz, would weed onions with only her right hand in the mornings, keeping her left behind her back, so she would have a clean hand to eat her sandwich at lunchtime. We still laugh about it. That's the type of situation and decision-making we faced. It was simple and rational, for the most part.

Thanks to my parent's hard work and some of our own, all three of us made it through college. We had choices. I moved eighteen times and have held twenty-five different jobs. My mom, bless her soul, never really understood what I did and was afraid I couldn't hold a job because

I moved so frequently. She and my dad actually came to visit us when we lived in Mexico City, and she insisted on bringing several steaks. I don't know why she thought we didn't have good meat in Mexico.

The level of complexity of my life eventually became too great for her to relate. Her mental model was, of course, built around her relatively simple life. As discussed in chapter 2, a mental model is a type of representation of the surrounding reality that we use in decision-making. It helps us anticipate what will happen in response to our actions. Her mental model was, of course, built around her day-to-day life. Our respective realities didn't overlap much, so my mental model was different.

To my mother, my life was complicated. It had many, many more parts than hers. Early in my career, we would talk about it, and it was not too difficult for her to understand my answer to her favorite opening question in our weekly phone calls: "What are you up to?" It was a stretch, but she could relate in those early days. But as numbers of jobs and number of new locations piled up, it just got too complicated. Adding many parts to a situation transitions it from simple to complicated. However, even when it became complicated, it was predictable. I would add yet another job and another move.

I had a different perspective entirely. To me, my life was beyond complicated. It was complex. To me, it was not just all the jobs and moves that made up my life—it was the freedom of action that I and the key players in my life had. Because of the combination of education, ambition, and hard work, I had many choices. As importantly, everyone and everything around me had freedom of action that affected both me and them. My parents did not have much freedom of action, and neither did the surrounding people. The biggest elements in their lives with strong freedom of action revolved around the weather, the size of their crop, and the market price for onions, which determined their income.

Today, most of our lives require us to be adaptive because the pace of change is high, and change is both commonplace and unpredictable. Our lives require us to adapt our mental models of how things work regularly as we make decisions to change or reinvent ourselves.

When we behave *adaptively* and things don't go as we anticipated, we learn the decisions we made did not get us the desired result. We adjust our mental models accordingly. As I moved from the farm to Syracuse University and then up the corporate ladder at Citibank and American Express, success depended on this adaptation process, particularly through my fourteen years in Latin America when I was fortunate to rise to senior levels of management. Adaptation is a critically important attribute as we move into higher and higher levels of situational complexity.

At times, gratefully infrequently, I would go over the *edge of chaos* (see diagram 1) and into the *abyss of chaos*. This situation is as the name implies. It is beyond out of control. With complex situations, if we're sufficiently adaptive, patterns emerge and our mental models adjust to become stronger in a Darwinian sense. There's nothing positive about the state of chaos except the possibility of getting back to surfing the edge of it, which is not an easy task once you've dumped your board.

Here is one more lesson in complexity to help in overstanding. Is chess complicated or complex? What do you think? Yes, it's complex? No, it's not?

The answer is both yes and no. The game itself is extremely complicated. Claude Shannon estimated the lower bound on the "game-tree complexity" of chess at roughly 1043. Called the Shannon Number, it is ten followed by forty-three zeros. Now that's complicated because there are an unbelievably large number of parts.

Okay, so it's complicated. How is it complex too? As soon as you have an opponent, it's complex. Why? Because then there is freedom of action, both for you and for your opponent. Once that happens, the moves are interconnected and interdependent. Your move depends on your opponent's move and your perception of your opponent's strategy. There is an interdependency of their next move on yours and so on. The level of predictability is low. It would be rare indeed for two chess players to play the exact same game against each other. There would be adaptation and emergent behavior. I'll spend more time on that later.

Below are some heuristics on playing chess quoted directly from an instruction manual. As you review them, think about how different people would come to different conclusions as they followed each of the steps to determine their move.

- Review the position and choose tentative candidate moves.

- As a rule, take the most promising play and analyze it. If it leads to a desired outcome, make it. (If you have enough time, analyze a few others to see if any of them promise something better.) If the outcome is unsatisfactory or unclear, begin to analyze the next-most-appealing candidate move.

- Keep mental notes on your discoveries as you go along. The "tricks" in one move will often lead to other strategic considerations and may sometimes suggest a new candidate to consider.

- When your intuition tells you that there might be a forcing combination in the position, but your analysis can't make it work, try brainstorming techniques like reversing the order and using what-if thinking.

- In a timely fashion, make a decision—and then double-check it.

Even if you are not a chess player, it's pretty clear how variations in the decision-maker's ability as well as their assessment of the opponent's ability and strategy will make substantial differences in the choice of the next move. Even with the same player, variations in other things that might be going on in their lives (their feelings about their opponent, how important the match is, what mood the decision-maker is in, etc.) may cause variations in the final decision. All this is also true for the opponent as they decide how to respond. That is complex.

Back to the workplace, here is the last lesson in complexity, this time from history. In the early 1600s, Adam Smith put forth a hypothesis that proved to be the foundation of the Industrial Revolution. In his seminal work, *An Inquiry into the Nature and Causes of the Wealth of Nations,* he described the impact of division of labor through a story about how efficiency would be maximized in a pin factory.

He postulated that if the eighteen-step process of making a pin (drawing the wire, straightening it, cutting it, creating a point, making the head, etc.,) were divided among ten workers, each specializing in one or two steps, a factory would produce about forty-eight thousand pins per day. However, if each of those ten people were tasked with making pins by themselves, they would make less than 1 percent of that volume. Much later, Henry Ford applied Smith's concept to the mass production of automobiles. It is still applied today by Foxconn in the manufacture of the iPhone and other electronic devices.

All this incredible economic development happened within the constraints of a complicated situation. While its complexity increased over time, its nature stayed fundamentally the same. It may have become complex at the margin, but, by treating it as complicated, the approximation was good enough to work well.

Through the Industrial Revolution and most of the twentieth century, we perfected our techniques to master the complicated. In the sciences, business, and elsewhere, we became adept at maximizing results by managing things as if they were complicated and not complex.

Karl Marx came along some three hundred and fifty years after Smith and contended that Smith missed the point. He believed that specialized work causes workers to become disconnected from their jobs as their work moves farther and farther away from the end product. The meaningfulness of work would decline, Marx argued, to the point it would have significant negative impact on the attitude of workers toward life.

I worked several summers during vacation from college for Ford Motor Company in what was, at the time, the largest automotive assembly plant under one roof in the world. I backfilled for regulars who were on vacation, and every two weeks or so, my job changed. I got to do all kinds of things from fastening bumpers onto trucks to hoisting engines onto frames as they moved down the assembly line to unloading boxcars.

With each job change, I had to learn an entirely new routine. This was challenging for the first day, but by midmorning of the second day, I would have it down well enough to start daydreaming. I couldn't have cared less about the meaning of my work. I was totally into personal economic development: making more than three times the minimum wage as a temporary member of the United Auto Workers union. Score: Smith 1, Marx 0.

But, driven by technology, things have changed a lot. Automation, manufacturing moving to low labor cost markets, and the rise of the knowledge economy all have been game changers, particularly the last phenomenon. Now, meaningfulness of work is key. Worker engagement is critical to success. A key challenge for leadership is to establish context. This helps establish purpose for employees. The bottom line is Karl Marx was right; he was just ahead of his time. Game, set, match—Marx.

Complexity and Problems

Houston, we've had a problem here.

—James A. Lovell

Making a decision is all about changing the state of a situation from its current state to some desired state. Effecting that change presents a problem. So, decision-making is fundamentally about problem-solving. Changing different types of situations poses different kinds of problems. In my depiction of this phenomenon, problems transition from transparent to translucent to opaque as the complexity of the situation increases from simple/complicated to complex and finally to chaotic (see diagram 2 below).

DIAGRAM 2

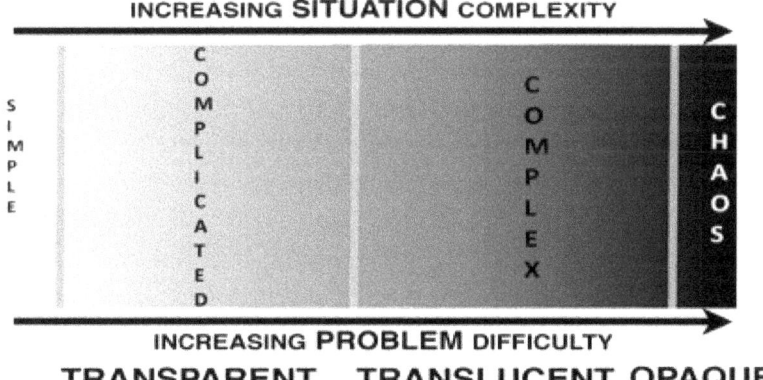

INCREASING **SITUATION** COMPLEXITY

SIMPLE   COMPLICATED   COMPLEX   CHAOS

INCREASING **PROBLEM** DIFFICULTY

TRANSPARENT   TRANSLUCENT   OPAQUE

Transparent problems can be clearly seen and are well-defined. The problems themselves are self-evident, and there is generally one right solution. Therefore, classic analytics enable stakeholders to agree on both the problem definition and the solution. Since they are like jigsaw puzzles, structuring the problem and developing the solution, while not always trivial (depending on numbers of parts/players in the situation), are in the realm of the known or the knowable. Trial and error is generally not required, though it may sometimes be helpful. Learning requirements are limited to technique improvements.

The nature of the situation and its associated problem are manageable, though how much difficulty of transparent problems can be high (building a suspension bridge or putting a man on the moon). The biggest challenge tends to be in solution execution. Parsing the problem and solving it in bite-sized pieces through classic analytical techniques is an effective approach. Strategies to make incremental improvement in financial performance, e.g., 10 percent revenue increase or 6 percent cost reduction, would typically present transparent problems.

Arthur Conan Doyle said, "Eliminate all other factors, and the one that remains must be the truth." The reason all this happens is because of the tight constraints on the freedom of action of the players in the situation. Once this constraint loosens, the complexity starts to shift from complicated to complex. The associated problem changes from transparent to translucent. That's where I believe Doyle's statement breaks down.

As complexity increases, associated problems become translucent (as shown in diagram 2 above). Solutions to these problems cannot be seen clearly because of the increased degrees of freedom of the players. Stakeholders will agree on the nature of the problem and the desired end state, but unlike a transparent problem, the best solution is unclear. Trial and error, learning, and adaptive iteration are required as the optimal solution is pursued. This is due to the interactive complexity of the situation created by the freedom of action of the players. Examples would include reacting to risks related to a new competitor's product, the risk of losing an important client segment, or deciding on a change-management program. It could also include reacting to opportunities in similar situations.

As the level of complexity increases and we approach the edge of chaos, problems become opaque. The freedom of the players in the associated situation and their interconnectedness increase to the point where the decision-makers and problem-solvers cannot agree on the problem. A working hypothesis for the problem and for a path to its solution can be reached only by consensus if there are multiple stakeholders. This is also true for defining the desired state itself.

All are subject to debate without a definitive conclusion. Trial and error with learning is required along the way to refine problem definition and structure. Learning is also required to perfect technique (as in transparent problems), refine problem definition, and adjust solutions.

This type of problem is sometimes referred to as a *wicked problem*. The term was first coined by Horst Rittel, a design theorist and university professor. Originally used in social planning, the term is now used to describe problems that are extremely difficult to define, no less to solve. Experts in the field will disagree on the very nature of the problem. Requirements are often contradictory and/or changing, and they are difficult to recognize. Situations associated with opaque or wicked problems have interdependencies that distort cause-and-effect relationships and create unintended consequences for action taken in the pursuit of solutions.

Some obvious wicked problems include the environment, American health care, and combating terrorism. Closer to home, strategic planning for a firm would fall into this category—and so would planning one's own career. Maintaining an innovative organization capable of surfing the edge of chaos indefinitely would also be a wicked problem for the likes of Tim Cook, CEO of Apple.

How Complexity Leads to Failure

Complexity drives failure in three ways. First, decisions related to complex situations and translucent problems are, by their nature, more likely to fail than those related to complicated situations. Just consider their comparative characteristics (complex situations are unpredictable, no clear cause and effect, etc.,).

Many of the situations we face are complex. It is just a question of how well the approximation works. Sound management and application of solid analytical skills can help contain the risk associated with the situation as long as the freedom of action is limited. As freedom of action and complexity increase, the approximation loses its applicability—and the risk of failure increases geometrically.

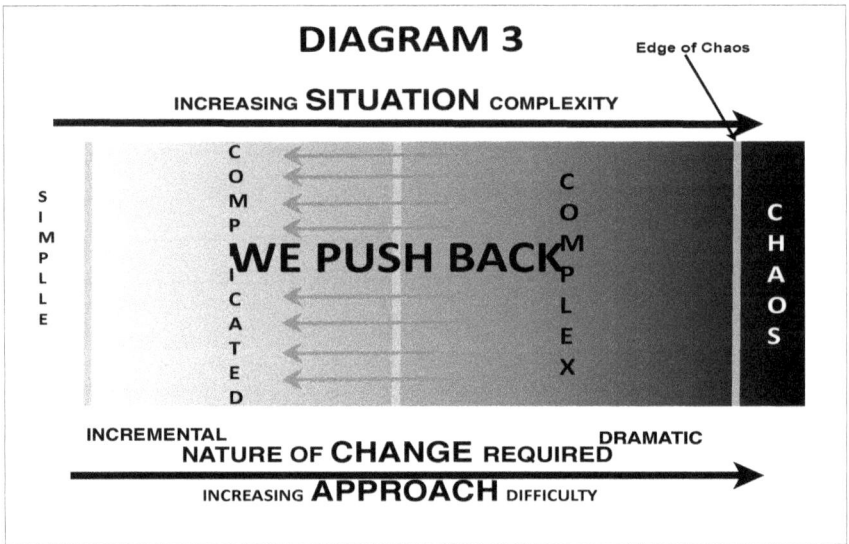

Secondly, we exacerbate the risks of failing by pushing complex situations back toward the complicated. This phenomenon is depicted above in diagram 3.

Tolstoy said, "I know that most men, including those at ease with problems of the greatest complexity, can seldom accept even the simplest and most obvious truth if it be such as would oblige them to admit the falsity of conclusions which they have delighted in explaining to colleagues, which they have proudly taught to others, and which they have woven, thread by thread, into the fabric of their lives."

Human nature causes us to want to treat complex situations as complicated ones. Complicated is where we are comfortable operating. As previously mentioned, this is where all our training and analytics apply. We look for rules-based, formulaic approaches. As we have already discussed, there is danger in applying them in situations and with problems where they don't truly apply.

We want to force them into our comfort zone where patterns are clear (even though in reality they are not), where one can clearly identify cause and effect (even though this is an illusion), and where we can seek predictability (where there is none). This sets us up to fail because our hypotheses will naturally be flawed. Unless we're lucky, our strategies will be erroneous. In essence, we are applying the *approximation* when it just does not work. Metaphorically speaking, to effectively deal with complex situations, one must bring together the wheel and the shaft used in dealing with the complicated and put them together to make a gyroscope. Said another way, we need to apply integrative thinking, which is a combination of intuition, reason, and imagination.

Third, complexity as a driver of failure is getting worse because, more and more, complicated situations are decreasing the farther away we get from the Industrial Revolution and the deeper we go into the information age. In other words, unless we get much better at understanding and embracing complexity over time, our rate of success in decision-making will deteriorate. We will be encountering more and more opaque problems. This is illustrated in diagram 4 below as the dark shaded (complex) area is substantively greater *tomorrow* than it is *today*.

DIAGRAM 4

TODAY

TOMORROW

Much of the explanation for this is the globalization of the economies of the world and the resulting interconnectedness. Also, success in the information age demands decentralized organizations capable of tapping into their collective intelligence.

How Not To: Case Studies

Well, I never saw it coming.
I should've started running
A long, long time ago.
—Chris Daughtry

The level of complexity of the situations we face often changes—and so does the nature of the problems. It follows that our approach to decision-making and problem-solving must change. The question is how to successfully navigate this labyrinth of degrees of complexity and problem difficulty. While the quote below was specifically written about GM, I think it applies more broadly.

> All empires contain the seeds of their own destruction. The ideas on which they were founded cannot adapt to changing times. Their wealth creates bureaucracy and complacency. Meritocracy gives way to an introverted oligarchy that wastes its talents vying for position within the imperial court, rather than expanding the empire's borders. Even as the empire shrinks, an air of unreality persists—right up to the moment when the Goths break into the imperial city.
>
> Mark Twain in Eruption

What follows is a synopsis of several situations where the inability to recognize and navigate the shift from complicated to complex and transparent to translucent drove success into failure. Alfred Sloan, an engineer and highly rational linear thinker, created General Motors through the development of a by-the-numbers, decentralized management structure. His senior management team was dubbed by some as "glorified bean counters" and "elitist accounting princes." At its peak in the early 1960s, GM enjoyed a market share in excess of 50 percent in the United States. Many will remember the following quote: "As GM goes, so goes the nation." Fortunately, that did not prove to be the case in the global financial crisis. While the United States took on water, it didn't sink like GM did.

By the turn of the millennium, GM's market share had declined to less than 25 percent. That was an extraordinary failure. But consider what GM did during the seventies through the turn of the millennium while Toyota and others were building market share. GM's situation in the market was shifting to the edge of chaos because its status quo, incremental approach wasn't working. It started to hemorrhage market share. Its problems were translucent—if not opaque—but it insisted on behaving as if it were in the realm of the complicated, managing its new product development and product quality as if it could dictate what the consumer wanted. Those days were long gone, but GM kept pushing back to the complicated. The results speak for themselves.

All this is akin to getting the deck chairs properly positioned on the *Titanic*. To make the point, then newly appointed CEO Ed Whitacre told a story about one of his first senior executive meetings at the company. He was exploring his team's concerns and aspirations for GM. One of the executives from manufacturing replied he worried most about "where the holes were drilled." He literally meant he was concerned about getting the holes drilled in the right places on the chassis. Needless to say, Whitacre was nonplussed by the demonstration of myopic thinking in the face of the recent catastrophic events (bankruptcy, government bailout, etc.) and potential doom (liquidation) for GM. Changes came quickly. According to Whitacre, "CEOs don't get paid to be team players; they get paid to be team leaders."

A second example of confusing the complex with the complicated is Hewlett Packard. Founders William Hewlett and David Packard both had master's degrees in electrical engineering and created a company with "innovation in its DNA." Indeed, innovation is literally the last word in its statement of values. Hewlett and Packard were brilliant engineers and businessmen, much like Alfred Sloan.

HP is regarded as the symbolic founder of Silicon Valley, having started in a single-car garage in Palo Alto, California, in 1939. It now has well above $100 billion in revenue, more than $5 billion in net income, and more than 300,000 employees spread worldwide. Their financial success since inception is unquestionable—even though stock price performance over the last decade has been less than stellar.

More importantly, when was the last time you heard of HP wowing the customer, any customer, with a new product introduction?

Somehow, as the pace of technological change accelerated, HP stalled. Though innovation is the last word in the statement of values of the HP way, it would appear to be more in name than in substance as a descriptor of the real culture, which is more deeply rooted in engineering than in markets. Purportedly, HP turned down its right of first refusal on employee Steve Wozniak's Apple I so it might "focus on the scientific, business, and industrial markets."

All the above is to lay the groundwork for the case that HP has been stuck in the status quo for well over a decade. The engineering focus on the complicated rather than the complex is buried deep in the culture and will be difficult for current CEO Meg Whitman to change. Splitting up the company as was recently done may make the task easier, depending on the moves that follow. I believe it will take years of continuity of senior leadership committed to organizational behavior consistent with nurturing a culture of innovation. Putting the word in the HP way tenets is necessary but not sufficient. HP's track record has demonstrated that.

My third example of a company wedded to the complicated when its situation has turned complex and its problems translucent/opaque is Blackberry. Founder and CEO Mike Lazaridis is another electrical engineer by background. There's a pattern here.

Blackberry had a strong market position in the smartphone space. It was dubbed the *Crackberry* fifteen years ago for its addictive characteristics. It relied on its global proprietary network and a quality device to maintain that position. It was a great engineering company solving transparent problems in a complicated situation, but it took its eye off the ball and was not prepared to deal with the market disruption caused by the iPhone. Subsequent new model introductions proved to be ho-hummers. Its stock price hovers around $10 per share, perhaps the value of its patents, down from a high of $200. Unlike Meg Whitman, the new management team led by John Chen talks less about innovation and more about the solid base of *engineering* talent. There's that word again.

He apparently will focus on keyboard-based devices, a strategy akin to a buggy whip manufacturer developing a two-pronged whip that will motivate both horses of the horse team together in the face of competition from the auto. There is already on the market a case for the iPhone that is a Blackberry-like keyboard that communicates with the iPhone via Bluetooth.

Chen, known as a turnaround artist, is basically expert at eking out maximum value in the short and medium term for shareholders through cost-cutting measures and supply chain deals like the one recently signed with Foxconn. These are necessary but far from sufficient.

In the long term, Blackberry needs to reinvent itself to effectively operate in the fast-paced world of consumer electronics. There's little in Chen's record to indicate he's the leader to take Blackberry from an excellent engineering company well-positioned to deal with transparent problems to an innovative organization equipped to deal with translucent and opaque problems.

The fourth example is Dell. Michael Dell had a brilliant idea in the 1980s that a manufacturer could sell computers directly at attractive profit margins, bypassing the entire cost of both the distribution channel and retail brick-and-mortar stores. He further leveraged that strategy by selling Dell computers directly over the internet.

While Dell is not an engineer by educational background, he would qualify as a geek. He got his first computer at fifteen, an Apple II, which he promptly disassembled to see how it worked. Dell's success was the hardware side of the same coin that Microsoft minted with its software. Dell was created as a manufacturing company and a successful one, but it is a one-trick pony. It is now struggling to learn new tricks.

Dell is an incredible cash cow. Market share lead in PCs has been changing hands of late between Lenovo and Dell. This is impressive performance for Dell. However, it is experiencing lackluster revenue growth because volume growth in the PC market has slowed. Michael Dell engaged in a protracted battle for control of his company with none other than Carl Icahn. That resulted in the largest leveraged buyout in history at $25 billion. Michael Dell, the winner, now plans to reinvent the company to enter the enterprise space in a model that will, in some respects, resemble HP's aspiration. Like HP, I predict a long haul. Dell is a manufacturing company with a culture built around dealing with the complicated situations and transparent problems. It is going to try to enter the complex arena. Michael has brought in some key executives with the right skill sets and has made some acquisitions with cultures more akin to his end goal than Dell itself, but Dell is still Dell.

The final example is Microsoft. Bill Gates, while not an engineer, would certainly qualify as a computer geek. He started programming in the eighth grade in lieu of taking his math course. He and cofounder (co-geek) Paul Allen created what would become perhaps the greatest cash cow in business history. Here's a quote from Wiki describing the early years at Microsoft: "All employees had broad responsibility for the company's business. Gates oversaw the business details but continued to write code as well. In the first five years, Gates personally reviewed every line of code the company shipped, and often rewrote parts of it as he saw fit." This sounds a lot like the way Steve Jobs ran Apple.

But then he turned over the reins to Steve Ballmer. Ballmer is a brilliant mathematician who scored eight hundred in the math section of his SAT and graduated magna cum laude from Harvard in applied mathematics. While not an engineer, he would seem to qualify as a linear thinker, i.e., one eminently qualified to solve transparent problems but baffled by translucent/opaque problems. Ballmer proceeded, over the ensuing fifteen years, to create a rigid, bureaucratic organization of dysfunctional fiefdoms. Reorganizations over the past couple of years are a Band-Aid applied to cancer. I believe it took Ballmer a dozen years to destroy Microsoft's creativity, and it will take years to get it back on track. It isn't at all clear that newly appointed CEO Satya Nadella, an internal candidate, is the person to get it done. He appears to be doing some of the right things, but time will tell.

The following is a personal example of confusing the complex and the complicated. A number of years ago, I was working with a consulting firm. We had the opportunity to pitch an engagement to a large Middle Eastern bank. Foreign banks were about to be allowed to enter their market for the first time, and the local industry was not prepared to effectively compete. Generations of complacency had made it bloated with inefficiencies. Even worse, it had developed a culture deeply wedded to the past. Product innovation was nonexistent.

Substantial organizational and corporate cultural change was required to prepare for the robust competition soon to be confronted.

It was my second time in a Muslim country. Many years before, I had lived in Iran. While I had long since outgrown the mental model of the small-town boy from a Polish Catholic onion farming village in upstate New York, I must say that I wasn't prepared for the cultural differences I encountered. I was fascinated by the strength of the commitment to the Muslim religion, the haunting call to prayer five times daily with the tradition of all Muslim males praying together at noon on Friday, the role of women (this was 1999), or the traditional dress. It all seemed so foreign. Riyadh is nothing less than impressive with its mix of the modern and the traditional. For all its beautiful skyscrapers, the manner in which justice was meted out was chilling. The food, while a bit exotic for my basic taste preferences, was excellent.

There was a team of five of us—four to pitch their areas of specialization and me to do the intro and wrap-up. We were ushered to the executive suite to meet with the CEO and president. Not surprisingly, it was sumptuous. The traditional tea was served, and after some small talk, we got down to business.

It was quickly clear the CEO and president/COO got it. They fully understood what they were up against both in terms of the desperate need to effect profound change in the organization and the resistance they would meet. The fear was palpable in the executive suite, and so was the sense of urgency. The two executives made it clear that the winning consulting firm would be chosen in consultation with the senior management team we were about to meet. While that boded well in terms of buy-in, it created concern as to what the agendas might be of the decision influencers when the choice was made.

Unlike the palpable fear in the executive suite, when we gathered in the board room with the senior management team, there was a sense of calm deference. All of them were dressed in their traditional garb of ankle-length coats (known as a bisht, once used as blankets when traveling) a large cotton square (ghutra) folded diagonally over a skullcap and held in place with a cord circlet (igaal). There was solemnity, but I got no sense of urgency at all. They didn't get it. From the pleasantries and room chatter, all politely conducted in English, my sense was that everyone was working hard to say the right thing in terms of being signed up to make change happen. People almost always say the right things in that type of situation, but neither the passion nor the commitment was there.

I had a sense of déjà vu. I had seen that movie before. I had starred in it. It wasn't pretty, and it didn't end well, but that's a story for a later section. This was going to be a difficult gig for whomever was to win it. The resistance to change was palpable.

We had, of course, done significant prep. Each of us had rehearsed several times in front of the other team members. However, I had an alternative wrap-up I had discussed with my colleagues as to its cultural appropriateness but hadn't rehearsed. It was there if the moment was right.

When our presentation began, I gave a brief intro of our approach and introduced my colleagues. They proceeded to present their perspectives and thoughts on how we would work with the executive team to get the job done. I watched carefully as they presented. I saw a ho-hum reaction. They still weren't getting it. I decided to go all-in, as the say in Texas Hold'em.

When it was time for the wrap-up, I said, "I would like you all to imagine you are standing on an offshore drilling rig. But this drilling rig is not in the tranquil seas of the Arabian Gulf. This rig is in the turgid waters of the North Sea. There is an accident, an explosion. The rig is on fire. The fire is serious—so serious that the alarms are sounding to evacuate to the icy waters of the North Sea. My question is, 'Are you ready?'"

As if I had a plant in the audience, one of the members of the senior management team asked, "But wait, aren't you here to tell us how to put the fire out?"

Now I had them. I said, "No, that's not possible. The rig will be destroyed by the fire just as your past ways of running your bank will be ravaged by the competition of the foreign banks that are about to descend upon you. Your only chance is to jump into the frigid, tumultuous waters and learn how to navigate them because that is the nature of the market in which you will soon compete. We're here to teach you to swim."

It went so silent that you could have heard tumbleweed drifting across the room. While I seriously doubted I had their approbation, I knew I had their attention. I then gave them a brief summation of how my colleagues' presentations were the swimming lessons they needed to survive and thrive. The CEO began to applaud. Others quickly followed, though they seemed bewildered why applause was warranted.

I knew when we walked out of the room we had lost the engagement. Professionally, I believed I had done my job. I had given them the benefit of my best thinking. I was not about to sugarcoat the task ahead of them. Too much was at stake—not the least of which was our reputation. Being a part of a failed engagement was far worse than losing the engagement. I didn't see how, given my professional judgment of the attitude of the senior management team, this engagement would succeed unless by some small chance they chose to jump into the turgid waters of the North Sea.

They didn't. I wasn't surprised. Another firm won the engagement. Measured by the performance stats of the bank over the ensuing years as well as by the bank's reputation in the region, the effort, like more than 70 percent of all change-management efforts, failed. Why?

I was as confident that the CEO and president understood the nature of the challenge the bank was facing as I was confident the senior management team didn't get it. They were too deeply ensconced in the way the bank had always done business to understand the threat they faced from foreign competitors with innovative products, the latest technology, and formidable efficiency.

In my experience, adapted from a Steve Jobs quote, there is invariably a brick wall of resistance to change confronted at some level in the hierarchy through which information does not pass in either direction. Change management stops at that brick wall and won't go beyond. The wall must be torn down, and almost invariably, that means knocking out some bricks. I had a guy who ran operations for me for a few years. He was a smart guy who was tough as nails when it came to getting the job done. He ran through brick walls. He used to say, "Bob, if you can't change the people, you have to change the people." It was one of the most important lessons I learned. You have to get some blood on your hands for people to believe you are serious.

Back to our examples, some of that bloodletting is apparently going on at several companies. The real question is if it will be enough. Again, this is necessary but not sufficient to effect real change. Only years of consistent execution according to the new model of complexity will transition the organization.

Here is a firsthand example of hitting that brick wall in a colossal failure. A number of years before the consulting pitch, I tried to push the complex into the complicated. This time I was the *perp*. I was put in charge of a division of a major multinational that had lost a considerable amount of money the year before I took over. This was to be a classic turnaround—or so I thought. I worked hard the first ninety days, assessing the situation and setting my strategy to solve what I saw as a transparent problem, and I set about changing the current state (losses) to the desired state (profitability). I had lived in the region for many years, working successfully in the same sector, and I was confident in my ability to analyze the situation and come up with a strong set of solutions. Did I mention my educational background was in electrical engineering? You can see where this is headed.

My strategy had three prongs, two of which were pertinent to the business and are not relevant to the story. The third prong was the key to success because, without it, the first two would fail.

The organization was structured geographically, and the decision-making process was highly centralized and bureaucratic. What seemed to be trivial decisions flowed from the country organizations through the division office to HQ where they would wind their way through a labyrinth of staff personnel before they finally hit a decision-maker, oftentimes the company president. Our geography included some volatile emerging market economies. Things changed fast, and speed in decision-making was key to being sufficiently nimble to keep pace with the economic environment.

Our decisions all too often became irrelevant before they were made due to changed economic conditions in the country in question. It was clear to me that had to change. I boldly—and in hindsight, foolishly—set out to change that. I stopped sending most decisions to the head office and started making them myself. In concept, I had the support of my boss from a couple of discussions with examples. For my strategy to work, I had to take the ball and run with it. Backlash was inevitable, but I felt it had to be done and that I could take the heat.

I began pushing back decisions to the country level. I believed that my country managers would be delighted to have an increase in their level of empowerment. Everybody wants to be empowered, right?

The first resistance I met with was from the HQ staff. They felt disenfranchised at best and railroaded at worst. I went from being regarded as a cowboy to a renegade to an outlaw. I was a hunted man. The intensity of resistance surprised me. I was naive. I had been a staff person for many years, but I was not a career staff person. I was part of a culture where all the power rested in the hands of line managers. Staff provided advice and counsel. In a centralized organization, staff positions have real power. They also derive their self-importance from inclusion in everything from meeting attendance to review of decisions and input on their outcome. Had I consulted Machiavelli, I would have understood the king's court was going to be out to get me. They were, and they did.

Underestimating the reaction of staff was one thing. Worse, I totally missed how my own people, both line and staff, were going to react to the new decision-making process. Instead of embracing it as both a business necessity and an opportunity to grow as businesswomen and businessmen, there was passive resistance. Sometimes the resistance was less than passive.

In a country managers' meeting on the new strategy, a conflict arose between a country manager whom I will call Rodrigo (it was a Latin American division) and me. He was giving me a hard time about the business specifics of a particular decision I was pushing to the country level.

After a particularly tough interchange, I said, "Rodrigo, you're being belligerent!"

Rodrigo replied, "I can't be belligerent. I don't know what it means."

Resistance comes in many forms. I tried to railroad all of them.

Decisions were not made at the country level. That was risky, and I had not taken into account that highly centralized organizations tend to be risk averse. Nobody wanted to own a decision and be accountable for its outcome. Decisions were simply ignored. Of course, this was far worse than having the decisions flow up a bureaucratic and slow process. It took me a while to figure this one out. The staff backlash was faster and clearer.

So, I failed miserably. About a year passed without substantive change. It should be clear at this point that my failure occurred because I had confused a complex situation for a complicated one. I took a command-and-control approach. I unilaterally decided what needed to be changed and set about to make it happen, to execute. Under attack by staff and ignored by my own people, I felt I had no choice but to leave, so I did. It was a missed opportunity at best.

From Thinking to Doing

The first rule of life is also the first rule of business: Adapt or die.

—*Fast Company*

To minimize complexity-driven failure, first, like when you minimize irrationality, you must be aware of the nature of the situation. Reading this book will give you an edge in that regard. You will know what to look for to correctly identify where your situation and problem lie on the spectrum. Einstein said, "If I had an hour to solve a problem, I'd spend fifty-five minutes thinking about the problem and five minutes thinking about solutions."

Think about the problem carefully. Most of us tend to be too solution oriented. We tend to attack problems with the opposite view of time allocation from Einstein's. That is the first mistake in approach that maximizes the chances of failure rather than minimizing it. You must carefully determine the level/type of complexity in your situation and thus what type of problem you face. This must be done by analytically (rationally) applying the criteria outlined above.

After taking the requisite fifty-five minutes to determine the nature of the situation and the problem, if you are fortunate enough to conclude your situation is complicated and your problem is therefore transparent, then by all means treat it as such. Apply all your classic analytics and management techniques. Look for cause-and-effect relationships and use them to predict the behavior or your situation and solutions to your problems. If senior management knows what to do, then set about creating and managing an organization built for compliance. Don't operate your organization at or near the edge of chaos if your situation doesn't require it. It is much simpler and more effective to treat complicated situations as such. Just be sure that your assessment is indeed rational.

Linear thinkers are great at managing complicated situations. If you are not an engineer or highly quantitative, find someone who is and give them a key role in your organization. Be sure to listen to them carefully. Remember, they are there to bridge a gap in your strengths. Also, if you are on this path, you need to keep vigilantly looking over your shoulder to ensure that, should the complexity of your situation begin increasing, you will become aware of it quickly and respond to it accordingly. The best way to do this is with a vigilant, ongoing process of scenario planning. This will be discussed at some length in the chapter on uncertainty (chapter 4).

Catching this shift from the complicated to the complex will take a highly disciplined team effort. Even the best and the brightest do not succeed at it as noted in the case studies above. A major part of the issue is the characteristics of a culture that is highly successful in complicated situations are not well conditioned for the recognition of imminent disruptions. Management continues to focus on transparent problems while ignoring the translucent and opaque problems looming on the horizon—or, worse, staring them in the face. Vested interests in the status quo rise with success and the firm tends to become rigid and often *siloed*.

One of the techniques that are useful in dealing with high-complexity situations is simple trial and error. Tim Harford describes the technique well in *Adapt: Why Success Always Starts with Failure*. Once you start moving up the complexity scale, well before entering the complex, step away from "the God complex" as Harford calls it. This malady is a mind-set. It causes you to believe if you can just find the right smart people, they will know the solution to your problem. With complex situations, that doesn't work nearly as well as the systematic application of trial and error.

Here's a case study demonstrating the power of trial and error with a complicated problem. Harford describes a situation where a detergent manufacturer needed a nozzle design that would optimize the process of spraying liquid detergent to turn it into powder. The firm hired a few expert physicists and mathematicians and had them produce the ideal design. It failed miserably. So, the firm took that design and made ten adaptations of it, picked the one of the ten that worked best, made ten adaptations of it, and so on. The firm did that process of adaptation forty-five times before it came up with a nozzle that delivered great results. It looked like a chess piece, and nobody could explain why it worked as well as it did. This was a transparent problem within a complicated situation. It was not a situation where the players had any freedom of action.

The God complex predicted the experts would come up with the right solution. It didn't happen. The situation was deceptive. It appeared simple, but it was highly complicated. Trial and error was the only way to effectively solve it. The power of trial and error increases as complexity increases. It is a key approach to satisficing when facing opaque/wicked problems.

Another key lesson on handling complexity is derived directly from the previous case studies (and depicted in diagram 5 below). The engineering and analysis that are required to deal with complicated situations decline as complexity increases and design thinking is required to achieve success. Engineering and analysis are well understood, but design thinking may be less clear. It borrows from processes used in creating new products or services, but—more broadly—it is useful in problem-solving, and it is used with increasing frequency to take on opaque (wicked) problems when innovation is required.

Diagram 5

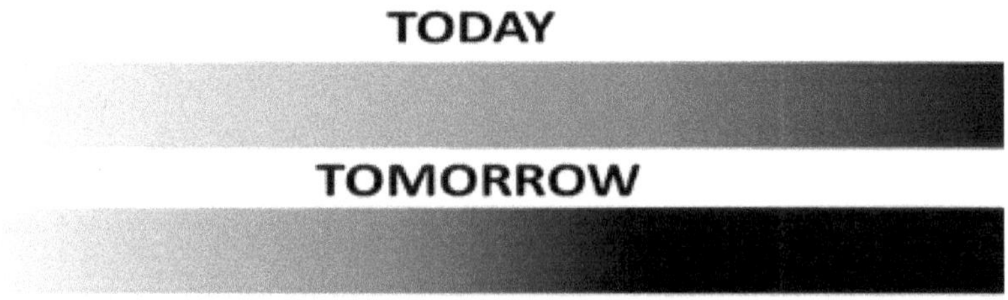

TODAY

TOMORROW

Crossing that line from engineering to design thinking is difficult but doable with some work. Design thinking is a different way of thinking from that taught to MBAs. It requires taking important steps toward creativity and innovation, but it's not the same as design. Design is an endowed capability enhanced over decades by training and practice. Examples of iconic designers include Jonathan Ive (Apple), James Dyson (Dyson's), and Phillipe Starck (Yoo Design). Jonathan Ive said, "I design and make. I can't separate the two." Note the footnoted title of the article contains the word *process*. This connotes it is something that can be articulated and replicated. Design thinking is all about enabling those not necessarily endowed with world-class creativity to replicate the process instinctively applied by designers.

It is much easier to successfully build a first-class engineering company that is a well-oiled machine than it is to build one that delivers first-class innovation. The reasons are straightforward. Engineering plays to all our learned skills. Building these kinds of companies is what MBAs learn how to do. It's also about command and control and hierarchical structures. As such, it is in the heart of our comfort zone. It is great if it fits your situation. If it doesn't, you will incur a high probability of failure.

Design thinking is not a process that lends itself to hierarchical structures or a command-and-control approach. Quite the contrary. Design thinking is a collaborative process that is generally built around small, highly focused, and interdisciplinary teams. It is a process replicable without being dependent on design geniuses like the iconic figures mentioned previously. Design thinking as applied to problem-solving is not some endowed capability. Design thinking is a skill—a process that can be learned—but it is much more than that.

Design thinking needs to be an integral part of the culture of the organization. Kate Canales, director of design and innovation programs at Southern Methodist University, said, "We just need to be supported creatively, especially at work. Creativity in the workplace requires context. At work, creativity is not a personality trait. It arises out of an ecosystem." That ecosystem needs to be characterized by action words like *foster, nurture, collaborate, encourage, safe to question, make, test, fail, learn, seek,* and *succeed.* It is an environment where the Silicon Valley mantra of "fail early, fail often" (add "fail cheap" through prototyping) rules. That is the environment where translucent and opaque problems are best tackled.

In many respects, the design-thinking ecosystem is another way of describing "surfing the edge of chaos." It is the healthiest place to operate in highly complex situations. There will be failure, but in a positive sense, that failure leads to learning and adaptation of one's mental model. Innovation is at the heart of the edge of chaos. Emergent behavior is key. Attempting control will almost inevitably lead to failure because, in highly complex/chaotic situations, nobody is smart enough to *know* what needs to be done. There is no room for Tim Harford's God complex.

The concepts for dealing with the situations at the highest level of complexity come from complexity science and chaos theory. In complexity science, the basis of discussion is systems rather than situations, but it's not hard to translate. Here is an adaptation of a formal definition of a complex adaptive system: a complex adaptive system is made up of independent agents that act in parallel, following a simple rule set, and develop "models" of how things work in their environment, and, most importantly, refine those models through learning and adaptation.

Here is a translation into our jargon: A complex adaptive situation is one with a group of players (could be large or small) who have great freedom of action (this is key), is guided by its culture (behavioral norms and values), and has a view on how things work in its environment (mental model) that, through trial and error, tests the environment, learns from failure, strengthens, and innovates. What must be added is the need for a common understanding of the problem, established either by a leader or by the group of players. Without that, chaos is likely to ensue. Also, problem definition is a dynamic process because, almost invariably, it will change as the situation evolves. The leader or the group itself must stay on top of this.

Complex adaptive situations also self-organize out of seeming chaos if allowed. Steven Pressfield said,

> "Chaos. The big bang. Crap flying everywhere. Imagine yourself back at the beginning of time. The universe is raw energy,

blasting faster than light-speed in all directions. (Stay with me, this is going somewhere). What happens? As time passes— maybe only nanoseconds—electrons coalesce around nuclei. Molten matter cools; stars and planets form themselves into spheres; celestial objects find paths and settle into orbits. Order emerges. Gravity exerts its pull. Rivers form and run downhill. Seas arise. Atmospheres stabilize. Before you know it, we've got adventurous fish crawling out onto dry land, hominids beating each other's brains out with sticks and clubs, and guys with pocket protectors doing IPOs for social networking start-ups."

The power of this model of decision-making and problem-solving is based on the properties of the interaction of the players. Emergence is defined as "a process whereby larger... patterns... arise through interactions among smaller... entities [players] that themselves do not exhibit such properties." One plus one equals three. The combined intelligence of the players invariably leads to stronger solutions to translucent problems, than does individual brilliance. Also, in highly complex situations, its process will come up with more compelling solutions to opaque (wicked) problems over time than any other approach.

At the edge of chaos, the players innovate through that process of self-organization. They leapfrog the competition, create disruptive business models, and wow the customer. They are high-performance teams in sports or in business. They are the millennial companies like Apple, Amazon, and Google. They have embraced complexity and made it work for them. They comfortably (or uncomfortably) surf the edge of chaos. They are led—not managed (more on this in chapter 5).

They are the opposite of Blackberry or even Microsoft, both of which are withering on the vine of innovation because they have become rigid and bureaucratic. Finding themselves in highly complex markets, Blackberry and Microsoft adopted the same fundamental strategy. They have endeavored to push back on the complexity of their situation and tried to treat it as complicated, which almost invariably leads to failure. It's just a question of time. Microsoft may be changing with its new CEO, Satya Nadella, but only time will tell.

For our purposes, perhaps the most compelling example of the power of a complex adaptive situation is the free-market system. If you compare and contrast it to planned economies, you get a good sense of the complex/edge of chaos situation versus the complicated. Consider the USSR as a classic command-and-control economy. Huge resources were expended daily to set prices and volumes of most all manufactured goods, and those decisions invariably led to excess production and waste or shortages. The whole process of resource allocation was controlled by bureaucrats acting out of some sense of common interest rather than by millions of independent and largely unconnected business executives acting in the interests of their shareholders and scrutinized by stock analysts and pension fund managers with the cost of capital, compensation, and jobs determined by the efficacy of their decisions. While the free market certainly isn't perfect at setting price and allocating resources, it is undoubtedly the best system known to man.

Applying complexity to the original case study from chapter 1, it should be pretty clear that I confused a complex situation with a complicated one. I wanted desperately to believe I had constrained the degrees of freedom of the key players on various occasions (existing shareholders, new shareholders, and potential shareholders).

Had I *overstood* the concept of complexity at the time, it would have been clear to me that there was substantial freedom on the part of all stakeholders and that I needed to act accordingly. Looking over my shoulder, expecting the unexpected, I would have created more robust strategies, always with a plan B. Contingency planning is a must for dealing effectively with bad assumptions, which is always a real possibility. In fact, they are far more likely than not. Instead, I was caught flat-footed—and so were my colleagues up the chain of command. That was hardly smart career management.

Closer to Home Today

A company (Harvard) must stay the course even in times of upheaval, while constantly improving and extending its distinctive positioning.[6]

—Michael Porter

---

6   "Business School, Disrupted," Jerry Useem, *New York Times*, May 31, 2014.

What they're (Harvard) doing is, in my language, a sustaining innovation, akin to Kodak introducing better film, circa 2005. It's not truly disruptive.[7]

—*Clayton Christiansen*

As a wrap-up to this chapter, I will turn my attention to higher education and its future. Besides being where I live professionally at the moment, it's clearly at the early stages of disruptive change. The above two quotes characterize the dichotomy that exists between two highly regarded strategic thinkers on that change. Under the Porter model, the disruptive change represents opportunity for incremental revenue through the brand extension. I think that is sound thinking for a Harvard, but for the rest of the system, it's not the answer.

The core business model must change for hundreds of private universities and colleges, or they will face bankruptcy. Harvard's Christensen recently predicted half of the United States' universities could face bankruptcy within fifteen years." This is clearly a situation that is screaming for the faculty and administration of each school to apply design thinking.

There are some parallels between this situation and that faced by the credit card companies when they irrationally rejected the opportunity represented by the proposal made to them by Rich Fairbank and Nigel Morris in the early nineties (case study in chapter 2). When Capital One was formed and began to take market share with pricing practices that attracted the best credit risk customers, the industry didn't respond competitively. It chose to bleed market share rather than responding with competitive pricing. Ultimately, it had to lower both fees and interest rates, but only after Capital One had established itself as the fifth-largest US credit card issuer on purchase volume. The big guys lost fee and interest revenue on retained customers—and also suffered dramatic loss of their best customers: high-credit, quality borrowers. If Christensen is correct, the fate will be far worse for the university system than it was for the banks.

---

7   Ibid.

CHAPTER 4
UNCERTAINTY: WHY GOOD GAMBLERS OUTPERFORM DECISION-MAKERS

The gambling known as business looks with austere disfavor upon the business known as gambling.

—*Ambrose Gwinnet Bierce*

Why is decision-making tougher than gambling? Because, depending on the game, in gambling, you can calculate the probabilities of winning your wager. In decision-making, you don't have that luxury. Your outcome probabilities can be guessed at or—in the best of cases—estimated, but they can't be calculated with certainty. That's why good card counters are banned from the blackjack table. They can and do improve their probabilities of winning to exceed the advantage that the house has. In some games, the calculations require a computer (Texas Hold'em), but the probabilities are knowable, at least to the TV audience because they're on the screen.

Decision-making is fraught with uncertainty, but in gambling, there is an abundance of risk. The famed Frank H. Knight described the distinction between the two terms as follows: risk is when future events have measurable probabilities of occurring, and uncertainty is when the probabilities of future events are unknown. Again, gambling entails risk. Decision-making entails uncertainty—hence the name of this chapter.

Probabilities are both unknown and unknowable in decision-making. Knowing probabilities versus not knowing them is important because probabilities determine whether we are making good bets or bad bets. As the names imply, you want to make good bets and avoid bad bets. What are the differences between good bets and bad bets? Some would say that good bets are the ones you win and bad bets are the ones you lose. I would argue differently. Reaching into the field of probabilities and statistics, I would suggest a good bet is one with a positive *expected value*.

Mathematically, a Dutch mathematician named Jacob Bernoulli developed the simple definition of expected value in the seventeenth century. It is the product of the probability of an outcome times the value of that outcome minus the probability the outcome doesn't occur times the loss associated with that outcome. If that number is positive, it's a good bet. If it's negative, it's a bad bet. If it's zero, it's a fair bet (neither outcome has an advantage).

The first point is that, in gambling, you can calculate the expected value of a bet because you can calculate the probability of the desired outcome—and the reward of that outcome is known. Therefore, you can determine if you are making a good bet (positive expected value) or a bad bet (negative expected value). In decision-making, you can only make these calculations with an estimate based on assumptions and not with a known number.

Why is all that important? Because, in gambling, the pros make good bets and avoid bad bets. Of course, they make good bets that they lose, but over time, they will be winners because they are making good bets with positive expected values. That way, you improve the odds of your emerging victorious. That's what makes professional gambling possible.

You go to know when to hold 'em
Know when to fold 'em.
Know when to walk away
Know when to run.

—Kenny Rogers

What this means is that, at the margin, when the decision-maker and the gambler make the next incremental bet, gamblers have a better chance of making a good bet (one with a positive outcome or positive expected value) because they know the difference between a good bet and a bad bet. We don't because we can't calculate the probability of being right. It's easier for them to know rationally when to hold 'em and when to fold 'em than it is for decision-makers. It's counterintuitive to think of gambling in that regard, but an understanding of risk versus uncertainty shows us the reality of that approach.

To put this in context, let me remind you of the track record of the pros in business and their self-assessed track record in decision-making. Going back to chapter 1, I refer you to the McKinsey survey I quoted from.

McKinsey has provided substantial coverage on the topic of decision-making. They conducted a survey of 2,207 executives regarding their perceptions of the quality of the decisions made by their company:

- 28 percent thought the "quality of decisions was generally good."
- 60 percent thought "bad decisions were about as frequent as good ones."
- 12 percent thought "good decisions were infrequent."

As I said in chapter 1, that's a pretty poor track record. Over half of those surveyed thought they made poor decisions 50 percent of the time. As I previously mentioned, this was a self-assessment with a natural bias to think of one's own organization as better than reality. That says, to me, that many bad bets are being made.

Of course, good bets can be lost. It doesn't change the fact that they were a good bet. The same is true of a bad bet. You can win a bad bet, but that doesn't make it a good bet. Why is that important? Because, like many other things already mentioned in discussions on irrationality and complexity, we tend to confuse things. When we make bad bets and win, we think those were good bets because of the outcome. Wrong! Worse than not learning here—we learn the wrong things. It creates distortions in our instinctive decision-making because we put the event in a pattern that's invalid. You can't judge a book by its cover any more than you can judge the quality of a decision by its outcome. You must be more thoughtful in your analysis than that.

All concepts have their limitations, including expected value and the insights it provides to decision-making. There are some decisions with positive expected value you shouldn't take because you can't afford to lose. Consider the following situation. A breadwinner in a household with young children, a mortgage, and a car payment is blessed with a steady job that she enjoys. She is offered an exciting position with a start-up company with great upside potential. It is the job of her dreams.

However, like most start-ups, the risk of failure is high. There are many, many things that could go wrong and very, very few of them will be in the control of our protagonist. What should she do?

Here's more pertinent information. She will have to take a cut in pay to move to the new job. Her compensation will mostly be in stock options that will be valueless if the start-up is not successful. Based on the steady employment she has enjoyed, the family (two children) had amassed considerable debt and didn't have much of a cash cushion. If she lost her job and didn't find a new one in six months or less, they risked probable loss of their house and car and probable bankruptcy.

On the other hand, the upside is substantial. Based on comparable situations, her stock options could be worth millions. There might be a life-changing economic event—an IPO or a buyout by a major player in the industry. She has a good reason to believe in the business model and in the team. The financial backing for the endeavor is strong and appears committed to the success of the business. She can't imagine a better opportunity than this. It's a dream come true, but can she afford the risk of being wrong?

She is confident that the probabilities of success are higher than for most start-ups. She has discussed this with knowledgeable disinterested parties and has assessed the odds of success at better than 50/50 whereas most start-ups are at less than 10 percent. Let's assume this analysis has all been done rationally (highly unlikely, but let's assume it was) and the probability approximation, while unknowable, is based on reasonable assumptions.

Based on a rational assessment of the situation, the expected value of the bet is substantially positive. What should she do? What would you do? Clearly, it's not an easy decision and one that only can be addressed personally. My guess is most of us wouldn't take the bet because the negative consequences are unacceptably high.

This is my final example of the limitations of expected value thinking that involves taking risky good bets (positive expected value) with a low probability of winning but with a large payoff. After exiting the executive suite of a couple of major corporations, I decided to enter *entrepreneur land*. I was in search of that life-changing economic event I mentioned earlier: a prospective IPO or major buyout. I had a clear strategy made up of five parts:

- I would look for gigs in the financial-services industry where I had spent my career and thus could add value.

- I looked for gigs with a proven business model and thus lower risk.

- The principal challenge would be to scale the business model to achieve both profitability and high growth.

- I followed smart money—the top-quality venture capital guys who had a great track record.

- My value-add was as part of a team of adult supervisors brought in by the smart money to take over what the young entrepreneurs had created and make it big and profitable. We knew how to manage growth and sizeable businesses.

I thought the strategy was pretty smart. My first gig seemed to fit it perfectly. It was an auto insurance premium-finance company that had come close to completing an IPO but backed off for technical reasons. It had demonstrated its business model and profitability sufficiently to attract $40 million in subordinated debt from the California Public Employee Retirement System (CalPERS—smart money). I was part of a four-person team of ex-Citibankers brought in by the smart money to clean, polish, and scale the business for an IPO. It felt too good to be true, and it was.

As we cleaned and polished, we found the losses embedded in the portfolio were substantially larger than we thought. That's not uncommon. Worse still, the business suffered from adverse selection; most of the people who wanted our product were people we didn't want to lend money to because they weren't apt to pay. If we tightened up our lending criteria to reduce losses, we choked off the volume of loans we were able to make and our cost to acquire customers went through the roof. In other words, the business model hadn't been proven out at all. The result was chapter 7 liquidation. Score: Smart Money and Sicina 0, Reality 1.

I was able to move to the next gig easily and without a physical move, which was rare for me. I assumed the CEO position of an auto loan business. We purchased loans originated by used car dealers through seventy-five offices spread across the US and collected them through three collection sites. We were owned by a successful "buy-here-pay-here" used car operation with a proven business model and a successful IPO under its belt. Its IPO was underwritten by a top investment banking firm. In other words, I was surrounded by smart money.

Our business was a separate division modeled after a highly successful "darling of Wall Street" that was trading at a sky-high stock price for a financial-services company. It was like I had discovered sliced bread or 7-Up. My strategy criteria seemed complete, and it was all there—financial services, proven business model, smart money—except the business model was flawed.

The smartest guys in a car dealership are called the "F&I" guys—finance and insurance. Generally, they're smarter than anyone else in the dealership except perhaps for the dealer herself. They are brokers. They make loans to car purchasers at an interest rate high enough to sell them to a company like ours. We would buy the loans at a premium above the face value of the loan. The premium was the dealer's profit. We made back the premium plus a profit over time by financing the loan at an interest rate substantially below that paid by the borrower. We had competitors, and so we had to bid premiums attractive enough to the dealers to win the business.

It became clear to me after several months of living the business that, as the industry grew, competition orchestrated by the smart F&I guys would drive those premiums up to the point where profitability would be unattractive. Growing the business only to be sold in an industry consolidation in the future made no sense. I convinced the CEO to close down the loan origination side of the business and put the portfolio in collect-out. In shutting down the origination, I closed all seventy-five offices in one afternoon via an orchestrated conference call. Score: Smart money and Sicina 0, Reality 2.

Next was a business that did home equity lines of credit equal to 120 percent of the appraised value of the house (high LTV lending). Yes, it sounds crazy, but this too was a darling of Wall Street. The business model, like others, seemed to be proven—at least in the short run. Underwriting standards were stringent but not stringent enough. The business and industry went south. Smart money and Sicina 0, Reality 3.

Then we had the consulting business we tried to build based on complexity science applied to organization design and behavior. This stepped away from my strategy, which was getting a little long in the tooth anyway. The end to this story has already been told. Smart money and Sicina 0, Reality 4.

That was followed by a child-support-collection business. The value proposition was for us to collect past-due child support on the hard-core cases for a contingency fee. The value proposition for the custodial parent was that two-thirds of some payment(s) from the noncustodial parent was better than 100 percent of nothing. It worked. The largest lump-sum settlement we received was from a New York Yankee, purportedly from that year's World Series paycheck.

The business was successful in Texas. Smart money (a top-quality venture capital firm in Texas) was backing the venture. It all looked good, but it just didn't scale. Once we went nationwide, the cost to acquire a client skyrocketed as did the cost of collection because the laws governing past-due child support and collection call restrictions varied from state to state. The business is still there—but at a size that was not financially interesting to the adult supervision team. Smart money and Sicina 0, Reality 5.

And then there was the idea, at the peak of the dot-com era, to use the internet to intermediate the banking industry and its consumer customers in Latin America. Latin America was an appealing market for several reasons: use of the internet was lower than many more sophisticated markets, so Latino banks hadn't yet built internet sites for their customers to manage their business; costs to acquire customers for Latino banks was high so a low-cost proposition would be attractive; and the revenue to banks in the consumer sector was attractive so there was plenty of it to go around. We believed once we got a few of the key players signed up to work with us, the other banks would quickly fall in line. For the consumer, we offered the opportunity to conveniently shop for the best deal.

There was plenty of smart money in this deal, including a top Mid-Atlantic venture capital firm as well as major players in the banking and insurance sectors. There had been close to $50 million of smart money in the venture when I moved in as part of an adult supervision team. We had not monetized any of our traffic yet when I arrived, but during the dot-com era, monetization wasn't the thing. Investors focused on numbers of unique site visitors and stickiness of your website (amount time a visitor stays on—the longer, the better). Revenue would come later.

It never came. The cost to acquire customers was too high, and the banks didn't fall in line the way we expected. We finally liquidated the business, and the shareholders got back about twenty cents on the dollar, which was not actually bad given most investors during that era got nothing back. Smart money and Sicina 0, Reality 6.

They were six seemingly good bets (at least they were to me at the time), all of which went bad. That's discouraging. So, I figured I might as well move to something I always wanted to do: teach. The pay was about the same, but there were no worthless stock options. How much bathroom wallpaper does one need?

What was the difference between me and the smart money I followed? They had a portfolio of a hundred or more investments. They would be successful if about 25 percent of those good bets gave the big payoff that I was looking for because those payoffs were big enough to give an attractive overall yield on the portfolio. It was much like John Wannamaker's famed quote: "Half the money I spend on advertising is wasted; the trouble is I don't know which half." The smart money folks were making good bets—they just didn't know (nor did I) which 75 percent of those good bets would go bad. I just ended up consistently on the wrong side of the dividing line between winners and losers. I had to do my bets one at a time, and I couldn't have a portfolio of bets.

Make God Laugh by Telling Him Your Plans

Embrace uncertainty. Get to know it. In uncertainty lies great opportunity. If you don't try to understand what's separating the known from the unknown from the unknowable, you're really missing out.[8]

—Hugh Courtney

Robert Burns said, "The best-laid plans of mice and men / Often go awry." I suspect it is only because of mankind's unconquerable optimism that we keep trying in the face of overwhelming evidence that the deck is stacked against us.

Decisions are made in the context of uncertainty. You can't get away from it. Like complexity, you need to embrace it as Courtney implies—not fight it. Embedded in every decision, implicitly or explicitly, there is the decision-maker's belief about the future. All of us are making predictions much of the time, yet the future is inherently unknowable and therefore uncertain. So, the stage is set for failure simply by being wrong in your beliefs.

Since uncertainty is always there, Courtney argues we should "get to know it." That's good advice. As importantly, Courtney's statement lays the groundwork for "embracing" uncertainty. In his words, we need to do this by "separating the known from the unknown from the unknowable." We do that by making assumptions, expressed or implied. It's our starting point in ascertaining our beliefs about the future.

In discussing assumptions, I will draw on the work of my colleague, T. X. Hammes who wrote an article on the subject that quoted an excellent working definition for assumptions below:

A supposition on the current situation or a presupposition on the

---

8. *20/20 Foresight: Crafting Strategy in an Uncertain World*, Hugh Courtney, Harvard Business School Publishing.

future course of events, either or both assumed to be true in the absence of positive proof, necessary to enable the commander in the process of planning to complete an estimate of the situation and make a decision on the course of action.

Before any further discussion of uncertainty, it is important to point out that the *known* in our assumptions can present important risks. This is because we are all too frequently wrong in what we think we know. What we treat as known can be, in reality, suppositions as noted in the definition above. Emphasis needs to be placed on *positive proof.* We cannot rely on the absence of negating evidence to be proof of the positive. It's not.

We need to revert to chapter 2 to expand on this. All our biases will cause us to hold onto what we think we know or want to know in spite of insufficient proof.

We hold onto our version of reality in the face of action-oriented biases, stability biases, and conflict-of-interest biases. Further, we reinforce that version with confirmation bias by latching onto whatever bits of information align with our suppositions. This causes us to likely misunderstand the problem we face and is often part of the previously discussed issue in chapter 3, i.e., pushing back the complex (translucent problem) and treating it as the complicated (transparent problem). Remember, these aren't suppositions to us. We believe these to be known bits of information even though they may not be right. Suppositions are for the unknown. That's why the known is so dangerous. It requires awareness of this danger so that close scrutiny and ongoing reexaminations are given.

It would be worthwhile at this point to review chapter 2 in the context of faulty assumptions of the known. It's important to note there are both suppositions about the current state (Courtney's unknown) and presuppositions about the desired state and how the future will unfold (Courtney's unknowable). Also, the process of establishing assumptions is typically an integral part of truly understanding the problem, particularly translucent and opaque problems.

All assumptions (suppositions and presuppositions) must be articulated so they can be questioned and examined. Presuppositions need to be reviewed for biases just as suppositions do and for the same reasons. This should also include explicit discussions of what might happen if the various assumptions prove to be incorrect as the decision unfolds. Does that cause one to rethink a decision? Will that cause a modification in strategy and, if so, how? As T. X. Hammes put it in his cited article, "If the assumptions are unexamined, the planners (decision-makers) will not evaluate the impact of being wrong and prepare accordingly."

So, assumptions are always necessary. You ignore them at your own peril. They are your navigational beacons. So, it is important that they be made explicit and therefore subject to the scrutiny of decision-makers and decision-influencers. Everyone needs to be playing with a full deck.

Isaac Asimov, famed author of more than five hundred books in nine of the ten Dewey Decimal system categories (everything but philosophy), said, "Your assumptions are your windows on the world. Scrub them off occasionally, or the light won't come in." It is extremely important that your assumptions made as part of a decision are clear in your mind and that they are explicitly articulated to key stakeholders. It is also important that they be comprehensive. None can be left as implicit because these then will be unexamined. That's dangerous. It's important to have contingency plans in the event that important assumptions prove to be incorrect. In these cases, alternate plans will prove to be essential.

The above are both sound advice and necessary exhortations because our instincts run counter to most all of it. In the words of Nate Silver:

> The most calamitous failures of prediction usually have a lot in common. We focus on those signals that tell a story about the world as we would like it to be, not how it is. We ignore the risks that are hardest to measure, even when they pose the greatest threats to our well-being. We make approximations and assumptions about the world that are much cruder than we realize. We abhor uncertainty, even when it is an irreducible part of the problem we are trying to solve.

Silver's admonitions ring true on many levels. I quote them here to reinforce the need for decision-makers to be highly disciplined in their approach to dealing with uncertainty lest they fall into one or more of the traps discussed.

Which Grain Will Grow and Which Will Not

If you can look into the seeds of time,
And say which grain will grow and which will not,
Speak then to me.

—*William Shakespeare, The Tragedy of Macbeth, act three, scene one*

Inherent in every decision is a forecast of the future. Forecasting is fraught with the possibility for failure. That's because the future is inherently unknowable. That's lesson one about forecasting. Nonetheless, some forecasts are better than others because some forecasting processes are better than others. That quality begins with your assumptions.

The second most important lesson in forecasting is you must make your assumptions explicit as stated in a prior section. They are the first and perhaps the most important product of your forecasting process. They form the context of and foundation for your forecast. Your forecast and how you use it in managing your strategy will depend directly on the quality of your suppositions and presuppositions. You need to keep a close eye on them to judge whether you are on course or not.

Here's an example where I got blindsided by taking my eye off the presupposition ball. I had a treasury unit that used most methods available to manage what was called *interest rate risk*. Our terminology would dub it *interest rate uncertainty*. We used fixed-rate debt issuance and various derivatives to manage our interest expense of our borrowings and thus minimize our earnings volatility. Our portfolio exceeded $30 billion, so we were major players in the interest rate derivatives markets at the time. So large that, in the early days before we understood clearly the interest rate derivatives market, the market would "see us coming" and move prices in a direction unfavorable for us. We had to spread our purchases over time to manage this.

For various reasons, one calendar quarter we needed to do a larger than normal volume of security issuance. As was our practice, we hedged the interest rate ahead of this volume to lock in the rate ahead of time and thus add predictability to our earnings. When you do that, those instruments will incur gains or losses in value as interest rates fluctuate.

Our presuppositions were that interest rates were more likely to rise than fall and so the derivatives would protect us from higher rates when we issued our securities. Our other presupposition was that, whether rates were to rise (gains on the derivatives) or fall (losses on the derivatives), we would issue the securities and amortize those gains or losses over the life (five years) of the securities. Accounting principles allow businesses to take the gains or losses and amortize or spread them over the life of the security as long as the derivatives were specifically identified as hedging those securities. Our earnings would not be volatile. They would show smooth and predictable growth.

Then things changed. We thought the market was unfavorable during the quarter for security issuance and held off. Meanwhile, interest rates dropped unexpectedly, and we started to accumulate pretty heavy losses on the derivatives—running into the tens of millions. Reality was deviating from our two presuppositions. Had it been just one of the two, there wouldn't have been a problem. We weren't paying close enough attention or putting the two deviations from presumptions together to see thunderclouds were forming on the horizon. We didn't respond. We could have cut our losses on the derivatives or issued some volume or some combination of the two, but we didn't act.

We were fast approaching the end of the accounting period for our quarterly earnings release. Since we didn't put on the volume of securities, those same accounting principles mentioned above required us to write off the losses at quarter end. Losses had mounted to a whopping $90 million. Our business was making about $150 million per quarter. A loss that size would have been devastating. Our external auditors succumbed to our entreaties and allowed us to carry the loss for one more quarter, but we had to do the issuance in the next quarter or write it off—all of it.

Our boss was apoplectic, and rightfully so. I had allowed myself to be blindsided and, in turn, I had blindsided him. The fecal matter was striking the rotating blades of the ventilation system. We needed to get out of the way.

In response, we crammed $6 billion down the throat of the market (more than two quarter's volume) in sixty days. It was surfing the edge of chaos for sure. We dug ourselves out of a hole that didn't have to be nearly as big as it was. We could have avoided the trauma and near tragedy of write-offs had we kept a close eye on our two presuppositions as reality unfolded.

Here's a story about forecasting run amuck. In one of my previous jobs, we had a disciplined process of budgeting and forecasting. It was tortuously detailed and rigorous to the extent it was conducted militantly. It was done as if the business managers submitting their budgets should know what was going to happen to their businesses in the next twelve to fifteen months. And it should be known in mind-numbing, excruciating detail: line by line and month by month. The budget was carved in stone in October of the prior year. However, in recognition that things do change, we had a monthly forecasting process. In December, businesses produced Full Year Forecast 1 (FYF1), line by line and month by month. There was a full variance analysis against budget. Each month thereafter, there was a new forecast prepared (FYF2 in January, FYF3 in February, etc.). But not all.

There was a communication process to preclude surprises. Any expected future variance to budget could not go in the forecast until it first appeared in a list of "Opportunities and Risks." Opportunities (revenue above budget or expense below budget) purposefully came first in this process because we insisted on optimism over pessimism. In some future month, generally carefully selected to manage both good and bad news, the opportunity became a *provision* and the risk became a *task*. When the senior executive decided the time was right to own up to a variance to the budget, the provision or task was released into the forecast. It was an elaborate and carefully orchestrated kabuki dance. It was all from extrapolating data buried in the general ledger of the businesses. It was single scenario thinking from targeted growth in earnings and then working backward.

Business reviews were conducted monthly, and they were brutal. The financial-control process cost a bundle. It was a large financial-services company, and the corporate controller once told me that the finance, accounting, and tax functions cost approximately $1 billion per year. Yes, that's right, $1 *billion*. And that didn't include the general management time spent on it—only the direct cost. This whole process was all there to create a charade of predictability in an uncertain world. The point of this story is that adding vast amounts of precision to what is inherently an inaccurate process only creates an illusion of predictability.

Modeling—The Science of Forecasting

Prediction is very difficult, especially if it's about the future.

—Nils Bohr, Nobel laureate in Physics

I spent nearly ten years as the chief financial officer of some pretty large businesses, some with net income substantially exceeding $100 million. As part of the job, I had to produce forecasts. Generally, mine were one of two types: lucky or wrong. Over time, I developed a philosophical approach to the job that was comprised of three parts.

If you must forecast, then:

- Forecast often. Eventually something you forecast will actually happen. You can constantly remind people of this success in the hopes that it will drown the many failures you're sure to have.
- Forecast long term.
- Avoid forecasting the short term.

If you forecast long term, it is almost certain that one of three things will happen:

- The parties you forecasted for will forget what you said.
- The parties you forecasted for will have left their position—and your forecast will be moot.
- You will have left your position—and the forecast will be moot.
- Forecast provocatively and with ambiguity.
- Say some things that sound intelligent and memorable, but give yourself plenty of wiggle room to be right no matter what happens.

Alan Greenspan was superb at this . In 2009, he said, "Housing prices could… stabilize or touch bottom… first half of 2009 *but* could continue to drift lower through 2009 and beyond." Say what?

Note the use of *could*. It's a key word for bringing the ambiguity to any prediction.

Please understand that these are meant to be funny rather than real recommendations. It always amuses me when my students write them down before I explain the humor. Having said that, Steve Levitt[9] was quoted as saying:

> So, most predictions we remember are ones which were fabulously, wildly unexpected and then came true. Now, the person who makes that prediction has a strong incentive to remind everyone that they made that crazy prediction which came true… But if you're wrong, there's no person on the other side of the transaction who draws any real benefit from embarrassing you by bringing up the bad prediction over and over.[10]

So Levitt would say that my guidelines first and third ones are good ones—not jokes.

Nonetheless, I believe Evan Esar described the bottom line in all of this. "An economist (CFO) is an expert who will know tomorrow why the things he predicted yesterday didn't happen today." On the subject of forecasting, a sense of humor is a must.

The most frequently used tool in forecasting is the model. Models come in all shapes and sizes. They serve a purpose as a starting point for discussion of the future in decision-making. However, they are all too often the conclusion of those discussions with the model's output serving as the basis for decisions. That's a mistake, and here's why.

If decision-makers can rationally conclude the situation they face is complicated rather than complex, modeling is a powerful tool. You will recall that one of the key attributes of complicated situations is predictability. However, as previously discussed, all too often, situations are complex. In those cases, while models are still important tools, they also have important limitations. Further, they represent real dangers

---

9. *Freakonomics*, Steven D. Levitt and Stephen J. Dubner, Harper Collins.
10. www.freakonomics.com, Stephen Levitt.

because of their potential for misuse. They may be a reasonable starting point for discussions, but stopping there is a critical mistake. Models are problematic because, by their very nature, they treat a complex situation (reality) as complicated (mathematical formulas, assumptions, historical data, etc.). The problems they introduce are described below.

The first part of the model problem is that we lose sight of the fact that they are an abstraction. They are an attempt to describe the essence of what's happening in the real world without trying to capture everything because that is not possible to do. The objective is to include the *right* variables, recognizing that you can't include all of them.

Models typically are made up of the following:

- assumptions about which variables are key (suppositions)
- assumptions about historical and current data (suppositions that they accurately represent the selected variables and thus describe the present)
- assumptions about the future (presuppositions of what the past says about the future)
- technical construction (mathematical formulas, simulations, etc.)

Note that the first three of the four elements in the constructions are assumptions. We have covered the issues associated with both suppositions and presuppositions. Among the various things that go wrong, some variables often get excluded that prove important. That is fatal to the performance of the model.

The technical construction of a model has varying degrees of sophistication. In general, the more sophisticated the model, the closer the approximation of the abstraction is to reality. But models are dangerous because, no matter how sophisticated, they are always an approximation of how things work, and they are generally built from an understanding of how things have worked so far. It may be fine-tuned with newly formed assumptions about the way things work and how they might change in the future, but generally speaking, these are presuppositions and not facts. Also, the more sophisticated the model, the greater the likelihood of almost blind reliance on it and its predictive power.

The second part of the perniciousness of models is that, because their output comes from a computer, we tend to believe it. This is what some refer to as the *control illusion*[11] or the confusion between precision and accuracy. We confuse a number calculated to five digits of computer precision with accuracy even though the first and most important of the five digits might be wrong. We confuse computers for crystal balls, and as Edgar Fiedler said, "He who lives by the crystal ball soon learns to eat ground glass."

The third part of the problem with models is that people who do not build them use them. These users are then unaware of the limitations of the model. Nonetheless, the more sophisticated the model, the more the user will tend to believe the output as a reasonable representation of reality. They become convinced there's magic in the black box. They may have a clear understanding of the variables included (or maybe not), but they typically don't have a clear understanding of the variables excluded. More generally, they don't have a clear understanding of the assumptions underpinning the model.

The Global Financial Crisis—A Case in Failed Modeling

An unsophisticated forecaster uses statistics as a drunken man uses lampposts—for support rather than for illumination.

—*Andrew Lang*

Here is a great example of models run amuck on multiple fronts. I believe there are at least five ways models were an underpinning of the global financial crisis that occurred in 2007/2008.

1. A key variable was left out.

2. Models assumed that decision-makers would act rationally.

3. There were severe limitations on the quantity of historical performance data of subprime mortgages.

4. As the technical construction of models increased in sophistication, users lost sight of their inherent frailty.

---

11. "The Financial Crisis and the Systemic Failure of Academic Economics," David Colander, Hans Follmer, Armin Haas, Michael Goldberg, Katarina Juselius, Alan Kirman, Thomas Lux and Brigitte Sloth, Kiel Institute for the World Economy, No. 1489, February 2009.

5. The dramatic increase in complexity of both economies and financial markets was underestimated.

For starters, the key variable left out of most Central Bank and other economic models was the banking system. Leaving it out led to two faulty suppositions. The first was the "Great Moderation" and the second was the stability of markets. Prior to the global financial crisis that occurred in 2007/2008, there was a consensus among policymakers and economists that we had reached a point in history of economic and financial growth, stability, and prosperity. It was a period like no other in terms of its promise. It was characterized by relatively high gross domestic product (GDP) growth, low inflation, and low unemployment. This period of the 1990s and early 2000s proved to be delusional, though it was supported by the best of the best economic models available. It came to an abrupt end with the recession of 2007–2009. It was then clear the Great Moderation—believed by many, if not most, key players to be a fact—was indeed a myth. How did the experts get it so wrong?

In terms of the stability of markets, a few hundred billion dollars of losses by financial institutions spiraled into five trillion dollars of losses in global GDP and nearly thirty trillion dollars in losses of global stock market valuation. Though many talked of a bubble in the housing market, no one's model linked the bursting of that bubble to a triggering of a global economic collapse. What was by and large missed was the necessity of including banks and other financial institutions as a key variable, playing a critically important role in the economy.

"'It's not just that they missed it—they positively denied it would happen," says Wharton finance professor Franklin Allen, arguing that many economists used mathematical models that failed to account for the critical roles that banks and other financial institutions play in the economy. "Even a lot of the central banks in the world use these models," Allen said. "That's a large part of the issue. They simply did not believe the banks were important." Hindsight is twenty-twenty, but it's hard to believe they didn't believe in their institutional importance in terms of the big picture. One might see how economists in academia might have left out this variable, but it is nothing short of astonishing that central bankers would have made such a mistake.

Next, economic models have, as an underlying assumption, that the players in the game are rational. Bankers will not take on financial risk that could destroy their franchises. In hindsight, this is an incredible assumption. While behavioral economics have begun to take human irrationality into account (as noted in chapter 2), the model builders hadn't yet caught up. You may recall *misaligned incentives* as a driver of irrationality. It's also a fancy descriptor for plain and simple greed. The drivers of the global financial crisis were fraught with it.

The third reason models were key drivers of the crisis was the limitation in the quantity and quality of historical performance data. These sophisticated models created the forecasts underlying the projected performance of the assets (loans) that supported the performance of the securities being issued. They were the basis for rating agencies giving AAA ratings (the highest possible rating and least risky) to these securities. The problem was that the historical data supporting the model was insufficient to produce reliable output simply because subprime mortgages hadn't been around long. The same was true of other forms of mortgages (low-documentation and no-documentation loans) that were being securitized. No matter how sophisticated the technical construction of a model, without robust historical data with valid suppositions supporting its relevance, the model's output will be misleading or flat wrong.

A fourth reason the use of models was a substantive underpinning of the seriousness of the financial crisis was that users lost sight of their inherent frailty. Senior executives in banks didn't truly understand the risks they were approving. They allowed themselves to be mesmerized by the sophistication of the models' technical construction. And they weren't alone. Economists, central bankers, investment bankers, rating agencies, investors, and regulators were all "smoking their own dope."

The fifth source of problems with models was that the increase in complexity of both economies and financial markets was underestimated. The capability of computers and their ability to handle massive amounts of data, and thus many variables, caused professionals to rely on them more. But the interconnectedness of the world's economies and financial markets has also increased at an astounding pace. In other words, models are complicated, but economies and markets today are complex. It's not clear the technicians' ability to model has kept pace with this shift in global reach and complexity. Like generals who are invariably fighting the last war, modelers are modeling the previous crisis. Models are, after all, built on history. Therefore, this increased reliance on the output of models wasn't—and isn't—well founded.

The house of cards was built, and it collapsed. Models are built on history, and history has its limitations as a predictor of the future. All model builders have limitations. This is meant to explain the role I believe models played in the financial crisis, but it is not meant to lessen the importance of other factors. Perhaps the wisdom in all this comes from Aldous Huxley: "That men do not learn very much from the lessons of history is the most important of all the lessons of history."

The Only Certainty is Uncertainty

Life can only be understood backwards; but it must be lived forwards.

—Soren Kierkegaard

It is curious that we persist in using tools like modeling and traditional forecasting in spite of their weaknesses to help us cope with an increasingly uncertain world. "It's all we have" is often a justification. So is "It's a starting point." The first is wrong, and the second generally ends up not being true. It ends up as the beginning and the end of our efforts to deal with the uncertainty. Hence, we deal with the reality of uncertainty poorly and unnecessarily so. As a backdrop for discussion of the future, I see it as made up of three elements as indicated in diagram 6.

DIAGRAM 6

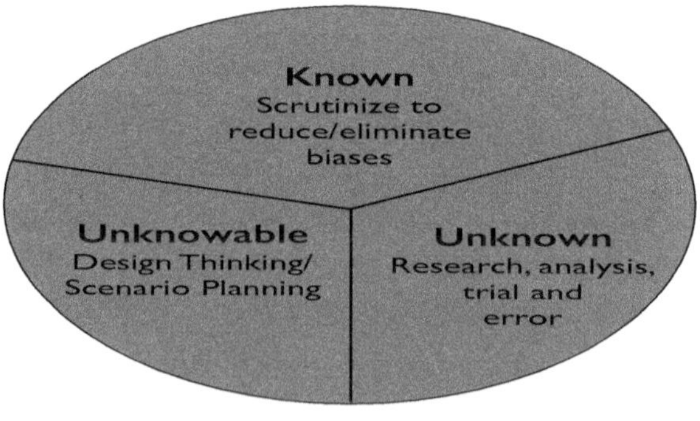

Known
Scrutinize to
reduce/eliminate
biases

Unknowable
Design Thinking/
Scenario Planning

Unknown
Research, analysis,
trial and
error

The relative size of the space designated for each of the three categories of information is irrelevant at this juncture. The classic approach to decision-making is to scrutinize the *known* to strip out any biases (as discussed in chapter 2). Then we move on to the *unknown* to determine it with classic analytical techniques. The unknowable is just that. However, while it can't be known, it can be explored. Generally, it's not. Therefore, insights that can be gleaned from disciplined processes, which include *design thinking* and *scenario planning*, are lost. Both are discussed later in this chapter.

In any situation, the makeup and mix of these three types of information about the future varies. This view highlights three traps that can lead to failure. If we don't recognize the importance of the unknowable, we pay it short shrift. If we do recognize it is important, we underestimate how important. We also reckon there is nothing we can do about the unknowable in any meaningful way. The right answer to the first is it's just wrongheaded thinking, yet we do much it because that's how business schools and the business environment train us. The second is wishful thinking. The third is wrong because there are disciplined processes that enable us to minimize the probability of it causing us to fail.

That is not to say that traditional tools are not useful—quite the contrary. They can be useful as long as their limitations are understood and their use is bound by those limitations. In the context of "Structured Thinking in an Unstructured World," I'll draw on the work Hugh Courtney has done on strategy under conditions of uncertainty. His thinking offers a helpful framework for dealing with an otherwise unwieldy subject.

Traditional forecasting includes tools already discussed like modeling of economies and markets. Modeling is also done of much simpler things like cash flows of investments, related present values, and expected values. Data collected for modeling or even less technically aggressive efforts would include competitive-landscape analyses, client surveys, and supply-chain analysis. All these analytics are necessary to ensure all knowable is known or at least estimated. What is left is the unknowable or what Courtney calls "residual uncertainty." Given Courtney's mix of risk with uncertainty, I'm going to cherry-pick my use of his thinking to keep my thesis clear.

Courtney describes four levels of "uncertainty."

Level 1

Uncertainty is low enough that forecasts can be used successfully. This is what Courtney refers to as a "clear enough future." I would describe this situation as one where the important elements of the future are either known or knowable. Established data gathering and analytical techniques work.

♣ Example: We will achieve X outcome provided we do Y.

- A reasonable approximation of the net present value of an incremental direct mail campaign can be calculated from historical experience.

Level 2

We can identify a distinct set of outcomes, one of which will occur. Forecasting and game theory work. "If/then" statements work.

♣ Example: If Epson lowers printer prices, then what is HP likely to do?

Level 3

We can bound the range of possible outcomes.

♣ Example: How will the next iPhone impact Apple's sales?

Level 4

Analysis cannot bound the range of possible outcomes.

♣ Example: What new products and services are going to be introduced by Google over the next three years?

Failure due to uncertainty tends to come for two reasons. The first is misidentifying the level of uncertainty in your situation, assuming it is lower than it is in reality. Returning to my story about the Catholic Church in chapter 1, I assumed I was at level 1 uncertainty. I was at level 2. This error in judgment cost me dearly. More often, decision-makers assume incorrectly that they are at level 1 when they are at level 3 or level 4. The second reason is simply that, at higher levels of uncertainty, the odds of getting it wrong go up.

Courtney argued in his early work that "level 4 situations are quite rare" in that the unknowable in a situation can generally be driven down to where there is a reasonable approximation of at least level 3 if not even a lower level of uncertainty. I'm less sanguine about that. I believe that, over time, uncertainty, like complexity, is increasing, so level 4 is becoming much more prevalent.

In his December 2008 interview with the *McKinsey Quarterly*, Courtney said, "We should realize that, across sectors, for most important decisions we're actually pretty far to the right (on his diagram of levels)—levels 3 and 4—in the uncertainty spectrum."

You will recall that certain complex situations can be treated as complicated situations because they are close enough to work without causing us to fail. This approach can also be applied to level 1 of uncertainty. Classic analytical techniques work well as they do at level 2, particularly with a dose of game theory added.

Level 3 gets more difficult, and level 4 lies deeper in the range of complex situations—at times on the fringe of chaotic. Classic analytic techniques are of limited value and are all too often misleading. Nonetheless, disciplined processes like scenario planning and aspects of design thinking can add great value to the process of creating a useful understanding of future possibilities. The insights gained can help reduce the odds of failure.

Courtney's work focuses specifically on corporate strategy. Since my focus is on decision-making of all sorts, the overlap is limited. Nonetheless, I will discuss briefly his strategy categorizations as they do have some applicability. Basically, he talks about *shaping* the future versus *adapting* to the future. If you are in a dominant position in your situation, you can shape the future. In my experience, that's infrequent. Sometimes when you think you're dominant, you're not (the credit card story with Capital One) and you've set yourself up for a fall.

Where you stand in terms of Courtney's levels will be part of your assumptions, just like your determination of where you lie on the complexity spectrum. In both cases, be sure to apply the processes to maximize rationality and to be explicit and comprehensive. Further, be sure to use those assumptions as you proceed with the execution of your decision to use them as navigational beacons. If you drift outside them, reconsider your situation and your assessment of uncertainty. Then reassess your decision.

Black Swans Cry Fowl

If you hear a "prominent" economist using the word "equilibrium," or "normal distribution," do not argue with him; just ignore him, or try to put a rat down his shirt.

—*Nicholas Taleb*

As Nicholas Taleb tells it, there was a time in history when Western Europeans thought that all swans were white. Then some Brits traveled to Australia and discovered the black swan. In *Black Swan*, Taleb adopted the term to describe events with three characteristics:

- a rare and unforeseen occurrence (an outlier)
- major consequences
- in hindsight, explanations are developed why one could have/should have predicted it even though it was impossible (retrospective predictability)

A classic example of a black swan would be the 2008 global financial crisis, although Taleb stated adamantly it was not:

> The crisis of 2008…not a Black Swan, only the result of fragility in systems built upon ignorance—and denial—of the notion of Black Swan Events. You know with certainty that a plane flown by an incompetent pilot will eventually crash.

However, Taleb has a strong negative bias against bankers ("banksters" as he calls them), and his abhorrence for bankers is expressed throughout his book to the extreme. Yes, the crisis of 2008 was a great example of modeling gone awry (as previously discussed). And in addition, as previously discussed, it was certainly unforeseen by economists, central bankers, bankers, investment bankers, mortgage bankers, brokers, and rating agencies.

Of the small handful who did forsee it, perhaps the three best known are John Paulson (an "event-driven" investor who invests in mergers and acquisitions and spin-offs, Courtney's level 2 uncertainty), Michael Burry (protagonist in *The Big Short*), and Nouriel Roubini (professor and economist from NYU). I would count these as having enjoyed a positive black swan (they exist too).

The other literally tens of thousands of interested parties—investment bankers, economists, and central bankers—were totally blindsided, which satisfied condition A. The consequences were certainly globally devastating, which satisfied condition B. In hindsight, all members of the financial community (banksters notwithstanding) pretty much saw that the housing market had to fall and that subprime mortgage lending had become risk-taking madness. Those understanding credit default swaps could, again in hindsight, see how the chain of events would bring big banks to their knees and so on. It was all clear in hindsight satisfying condition C.

That's the makings of a black swan that cried fowl on the predictions of the experts. Taleb's work gives other examples. Essentially though, his work is more focused on why we are virtually hardwired to ignore the possibility of black swans and to see all change as driven by logical incrementalism. Taleb spends a substantial amount of time in *Black Swan* explaining why we tend to disregard outliers—or substantially underestimate the probability of them—even though he contends most of the driving forces of change in history are black swans. It is not in our nature to discern the reality of the randomness within which we live. We (including the experts) suffer from the "illusion of understanding." We want to believe that black swans are so rare as to be irrelevant. Taleb says we're wrong, and I believe he's correct. Part of how we get tripped up in this is by what Taleb calls the "round-trip fallacy."

It goes like this. Nobody has ever seen a black swan, so there is no evidence that black swans exist. This is mistaken as evidence that there is no possibility of the existence of black swans. And then there's what he calls the "narrative fallacy." He argues quite persuasively that we all like stories because simplification and summarization make us more comfortable dealing with the complexity of real life. You will likely remember a related issue from chapter 3 treating the complex as complicated. Further, when we look at the sequence of facts, we compulsively weave a story line through them that force fits logic which, while satisfying to us, just doesn't fit with reality.

Much of what Taleb has written is about society and things that can be done systemically to limit the damage of black swans. I have selected some of Taleb's advice that I think is particularly good for decision-makers. The first is, as indicated at the beginning of this chapter, not to fight uncertainty. Embrace it and accept the reality that we live in an uncertain world fraught with randomness and black swans. That word defies prediction so beware of overreliance on established trends. Beware of the narrative fallacy and assumptions related to the predictability of the future. Remember that forecasts predicated by past events are inherently unreliable.

Next is to properly value *redundancy*. Taleb convincingly argues we undervalue "belt and suspenders" because we turn our backs on the existence of black swans or certainly underestimate their importance in life. He advocates devoting resources to *preparation* rather than *prediction*. Taleb argues this is in part because we don't fully grasp the interconnectedness of the world. He sees great risk in globalization that offsets the efficiencies associated with it. Most experts don't see it that way, but it is clear that there is risk associated with it. We underestimate it as we saw in the 2008 financial crisis. Since the forces of globalization are inexorable, redundancy takes on a high level of importance. Again, redundancy makes sense simply because we substantially underestimate the frequency and impact that black swans have in shaping history.

Also, when forecasting is a must, Taleb advocates organic or bottoms-up forecasting rather than a central, doctrinaire approach. Never overlook, however, that irrespective of the source, forecasting is fragile. Its accuracy degrades quickly over time. He goes on to encourage shaping one's natural urge to forecast around small predictions, thus "being a fool in the right places."

Taleb suggests that multiple small failures are inevitable and that these failures are a good thing. This fits well with the thinking I expressed in chapter 3 regarding the value of trial and error. This is also aligned with design thinking where an objective is to prototype quickly to learn. As importantly, in the context of black swans, this approach avoids exposure to big and costly failures.

The final point I'll make on Taleb's work is regarding *assumptions*. Assumptions should not be ranked in terms of their plausibility. Rather, they should be ranked in terms of the damage they may cause if they prove to be incorrect. Linked to this last thought is the probability of black swans cannot generally be calculated, but the damage they can cause often can and should be assessed.

Going back to my story at the beginning of this book of the Catholic Church and my deal to reposition the ownership of the bank, the scandal of Banco Ambrosiano and the death of Roberto Calvi most certainly fit Taleb's definition of a black swan.

Experts Discussing Expert Forecasting

When the train of history hits a curve, the intellectuals fall off.
—*Karl Marx*

Just so you don't feel too badly about your forecasting ability (or inability), the track record of experts isn't much better. Anecdotally, Margaret Thatcher, as a young woman, said she didn't expect to see a woman as prime minister of the UK in her lifetime. Ken Olsen was the CEO of Digital Equipment Corporation, the maker of the minicomputer that started the wave that upended IBM as the dominant "mainframe" manufacturer (IBM 360) some thirty years ago. Ken said, "There is no reason for any individual to have a computer in his home."

Evidence of the poor prediction track record of experts goes well beyond anecdotes. Philip Tetlock, a research psychologist and professor at the University of Pennsylvania, set out to track the decision-making skills of experts in the various fields from government to academia to journalism. To limit biases, he chose 282 individuals with varying points of view in their respective fields. Over twenty years, the participants made some eighty thousand predictions. The results were startling. These experts barely beat the predictions of the average reader of the *New York Times*. It was substantially worse than an extrapolation algorithm built around predicting the continuation of the status quo. Tetlock said, "The average expert was found to be only slightly more accurate than a dart-throwing chimpanzee."

Tetlock concluded experts think they know more than they do. He characterized many as being "massively overconfident." Forecasters with high profiles in the media did especially poorly. Tetlock also concluded the biggest single reason for their poor showing was "dogmatism." Experts with poor track records had singular beliefs about how things work in their fields. They approach forecasting deductively as a top-down exercise. They would not let go of these beliefs in spite of growing evidence that life was more complex than any single idea could accurately describe. Good predictors conversely tend to have high capacity for self-criticism. One sign of how good you are at this is how you handle the question: "What would it take to convince me I'm wrong?"

Tetlock turned to the work of Isaiah Berlin on the hedgehog and the fox to describe the issue. Berlin divided thinkers into two types. One was the hedgehog, which has one big idea on how life works (Tetlock's dogmatism). Berlin included Plato, Nietzsche, Dante, and Proust among others in this category. Next was the fox that knows many things. Berlin included Aristotle, Shakespeare, Balzac, and Joyce in this category.

Tetlock applied Berlin's characterizations of the hedgehog and the fox to his observations on forecasters and appropriately so. He concluded that hedgehogs made particularly poor forecasters while foxes did quite well. Apparently knowing many small things, being flexible, and adapting are far more powerful traits denoting accuracy in the realm of predicting.

As a high-profile example, I would put the famed Nouriel Roubini in the hedgehog category. Lauded by Taleb and many, many others for his prediction of the 2008 financial crisis, I believe Roubini fits Tetlock's definition. Dubbed "Dr. Doom" and "Permabear" in the media, Roubini had predicted a major crash in the US housing market and a severe downturn in the US economy for several years. Sometime after Roubini was given those monikers, *Forbes* said, "In 2005 Roubini said home prices were riding a speculative wave that would soon sink the economy. Back then the professor was called a Cassandra. Now he's a sage."

That's the upside of being a hedgehog. If your forecast eventually turns right, you're considered prescient. After more than a decade of severely bearish forecasting, the Permabear has shifted to a much rosier picture for the US and the global economy. On the surface, this doesn't appear to be any type of transformation from a hedgehog into a fox. More likely, he is still a hedgehog with a new, single idea. Tetlock's observations fit well with the lessons of chapter 3.

Certainly, the decisions being made by these experts involved complex situations for the most part. The predictability is low in these situations by their nature as already discussed. Hedgehogs would do well predicting in complicated situations, but—as I described—there are fewer and fewer of those. Their propensity to fail is due to their forcing an approximation of a complicated situation on a complex one. We know that the level of predictability is much lower with complex situations. Causal relationships are much more difficult to discern. Therefore, big, bold statements (the sound bites that newscasters love to hear) just don't work for the most part until and unless you finally hit one like Roubini did.

Further, rational predictions (Kahneman and Tversky, chapter 2) cannot be made as hedgehogs make them. Hedgehog decision-making is tantamount to instinctive decision-making and is irrational in complex situations because it rests on that single big idea. Rather than that, each prediction requires slow and deliberate consideration of the facts like the fox would approach things.

These observations on poor predictions go well beyond politics and international affairs. In the business sector, Christina Fang, a management professor at New York University's Stern School, and Jerker Denrell of Said Business School at the University of Oxford conducted a study of business decision-makers. They used data from the *Wall Street Journal's* survey of economic forecasts among other sources to demonstrate those predictors who correctly predicted a "big hit" tended to have a weak average track record:

> Intuitively, an accurate forecast is more likely to have been made by a forecaster who has better judgment and is better able to evaluate the situation. Here we argue there is a simple reason why this intuition may be wrong. Rather than being an indication of good judgment, accurately forecasting a rare event like business success may be an indication of poor judgment.

The reason is a forecaster with poor judgment is more likely than a forecaster with good judgment to predict the rare and extreme event of a product becoming successful.

Their thesis is those who correctly predict major, unlikely events operate instinctively without taking into account myriad available information on the subject. In other words, like hedgehogs, the facts do not confuse them. Those with good track records in prediction tend to carefully scrutinize the facts and don't tend to make big-hit or big-fail kinds of forecasts. These observations mesh well with Tetlock's findings as well as his observation on the hedgehog versus the fox. This also fits well with the work of Kahneman and Tversky (cited in chapter 2) on instinctive decision-making.

Michael J. Burry actually started off as a hedgehog and then turned fox. His big idea was that the turn of the twenty-first century closely resembled the Great Depression when some 50 percent of all mortgages defaulted. But Burry didn't stop there. He actually dug in and read the underlying mortgages of a select few of the collateralized debt obligations. He investigated some borrowers to discover their weak FICO scores. He investigated further and learned many of the mortgages had adjustable rates and teaser rates (some portion of interest actually accruing into principle) and would reset in the first quarter of 2007. From this set of facts, uncovered in a foxlike manner, Burry set out to short the mortgage market, and he invented the credit default swap as the vehicle to do it. It is rare person who can be both hedgehog and fox.

I have a confession to make. I am a hedgehog. I have been asked many times to appear on TV both domestically and internationally. I hunt for sound bites prior to appearing. My key source is the *Economist*. My objective is to be provocative. Here is one example.

I was invited by China Central Television (CCTV) America to appear on their prime-time live morning (Beijing time) news program. I was asked to comment on an Argentina dam project that, at the time, had a price tag exceeding $4 billion. When I received the call, I was unaware of the project, but I did have some strong feelings (largely instinctive) about Argentina and the weakness of its economy. Besides cooking the books on its inflation numbers for several years, it was maintaining an artificially high value for its currency that would have to be adjusted (devaluation) and rather quickly was running out of international reserves (its savings account was nearing zero). It is the only country in history sanctioned by the International Monetary Fund for incorrectly reporting its inflation statistics after repeated warnings.

A quick check in the *Economist* showed a story on the controversy regarding the water level on the dam project and whether it was sufficient to deliver the projected level of electric power. Also, the dam was to be in distant Patagonia, and the losses of power over long-distance cable were viewed by some as likely to make the dam uneconomical. That was all I needed to know. I was ready for the cameras after about thirty minutes of research.

Phillip Yin, the business anchor of CCTV America, did the interview on his show BizAsia. His previous interviews included International Monetary Fund managing director Christine Lagarde, World Bank president Robert Zoellick, Standard & Poor's president Deven Sharma, HSBC Bank CEO Peter Wong, East West Bank CEO Dominic Ng, and tennis champion Roger Federer. I joined this august list as Robert V. Sicina, executive in residence, the American University Kogod School of Business.

Phillip started with an open-ended question about what I thought about the dam project. Without hesitation I said, "I would describe this deal in a single word. Disaster. And I would put an adjective in front of it. Unmitigated disaster." Needless to say, I had succeeded in hijacking the interview. I went on to explain it was a "lose-lose proposition" because the dam would be uneconomical for Argentina, and China would not get paid as promised because Argentina's economy was in shambles.

Once the cameras were off on what turned out to be a five-minute interview, Phil remarked that, after my first answer, he was afraid he was going to run out of questions. We chuckled. It was clear he was satisfied; it had been a colorful and therefore successful job. This was classic hedgehog behavior before I had even heard the term applied to latching on to one big idea and going for the sound bite. So, next time you hear an "expert" make a startling pronouncement on the news, remember Tetlock's work and this story. Be skeptical.

Makin' Stuff Up

Forecasting future events is often like searching for a black
cat in an unlit room that may not even be there.
—Steve Davidson, The Crystal Ball

Given the challenges posed by uncertainty, what tools or techniques are out there to help us think through this major driver of failed decision-making? One of the most meaningful that I have found is scenario planning. This approach is best suited to long-term strategic planning. Books have been written on the subject that I will draw from. However, it is not my intention to teach you the technique. It is more to make you aware that it is out there. Scenario planning can make a meaningful contribution to your organizational efforts to understand and cope with uncertainty.

Scenario planning was first developed in after World War II. The Rand Corporation, a famous think tank, used it to develop scenarios during the Cold War. It is used principally for group-based decision-making. Unlike forecasting, scenario planning doesn't try to develop a prediction of the future based on historical data. It doesn't try to predict at all. It assiduously avoids deterministic views of the future.

Scenario planning is widely used in business. Probably the best-known practitioner is Royal Dutch Shell. They have institutionalized the practice and have been applying it successfully for almost fifty years. It enabled them to prepare for the fall of the Berlin Wall and a couple of oil shocks—well ahead of their competition.

But they are not alone. It has been said that almost no business operates without some kind of scenario planning. Over the years, practitioners have included companies as diverse as Apple, HP, American Express, Disney, and Procter & Gamble. There are others that would have benefited from applying the tool but didn't, including the financial-services industry before the recent global crisis, Research in Motion (Blackberry), and the Detroit automotive industry during the period that Japanese manufacturers ate their lunch (the eighties and nineties until their government bailout).

So, what is this beast called scenario planning? In the words of Peter Schwartz, scenario planning is "a tool for ordering one's perceptions about alternative future environments in which one's decisions might be played out." That's a good way to look at it. I would also add a good scenario plan must include challenging, plausible, and divergent stories about the future. But the final word on defining scenario planning rightfully belongs to the father of the discipline: Pierre Wack (Royal Dutch Shell). He said, "Scenario planning is a discipline for rediscovering the original entrepreneurial power of creative foresight in contexts of accelerated change, greater complexity, and genuine uncertainty."

When is scenario planning appropriate? In situations with high levels of uncertainty and complexity and when the stakes are high. Uncertainty and complexity are common to almost every corporate decision-making process so scenario planning ought to be included in some fashion. In the words of Toby Keith, famed country singer, "Cause if ya don't know where you're goin', you might end up somewhere else." In terms of the third element—when the stakes are high—scenario planning only makes sense when there is considerable effort, and therefore cost, at stake. This type of planning should only be undertaken when the value is assured.

When I think of scenario planning, the first words that come to mind are *disciplined process*. Yes, it's about storytelling, which sounds very airy-fairy, but—done well—scenario planning is a process that is fundamentally about change in the organizational mind-set. Yes, there is artistry involved, but there is also extensive data gathering and analysis. No, it has nothing to do with the normal forward-thinking corporate processes of budgeting and forecasting (generally a one-year time frame) or strategic planning (generally a two-to-three-year time frame) both of which tend to be rigidly structured in the thinking they produce. It's not about predicting the future. It's about exploring the future. It's about dialogue. It's about changing the mental models of the people (the way they think the world works) who are involved in the exercise. The end product, the scenarios themselves, are far less important than the process and the impact it has on participants. Royal Dutch Shell makes their scenarios publicly available. Here is how Amazon describes their book:

For over 30 years, the Royal Dutch/Shell Group has used

these scenarios to identify business risks and opportunities in ways forecasts cannot. Now for the first time these scenarios are available to the public. This book portrays three plausible futures with contrasting economic, political, and regulatory features and distinct implications for the energy system.

Admittedly, the work is a bit dated (it was done several years ago), and its time horizon is 2025. Beyond that, the work is brilliant, which is not surprising given the source. Consider it recommended reading.

Scenario planning is not just sitting around and making stuff up. It's a disciplined process, a learning process, and a mind-opening and mind-expanding process. The reason Shell releases its scenarios to the public—and thus to the competition—is because they know the real value of scenario planning is the learning that its staff get from the exercise. The following is one step-by-step approach (there are many out there):

- Stakeholders agree on a central question to be addressed. This needs to be thoroughly vetted and understood by all before proceeding to step 2.
- Identify the driving forces that are likely to shape the future. Generally, these will fall into the five major categories:
  - social
  - economic
  - political
  - technological
  - environmental
- Depending on the central question, other forces like competitive threats may be included. In completing this process, you need to look past the everyday to the long term. You need to transcend today's concerns.
- Plot your driving forces on a graph where the x-axis is the degree of uncertainty surrounding each and the y-axis is the degree of importance to the central question. An example is shown in diagram 7, which is taken from some work I did (discussed later in this chapter). Focus on those in the upper right-hand corner (high importance and high uncertainty) and

select the two most pertinent to your central question.

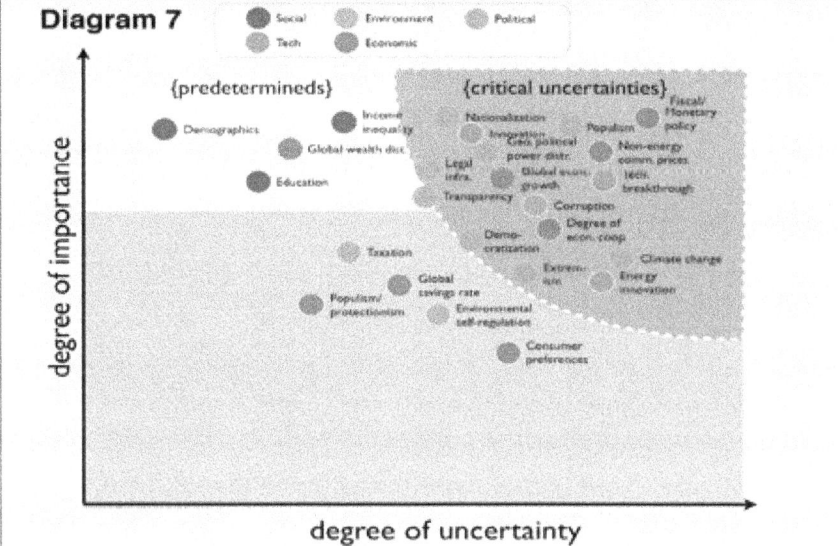

Here are the following steps:

- The two selected forces form your *axes of uncertainty*.

- Scenarios are then developed for each of the four quadrants. Remember these scenarios must be challenging yet plausible, exaggerated, and divergent. They should be like caricatures. They should also have clever names as part of the development of a new language within your participants/audience.

- Determine what the key implications are for the central question and the stakeholders. What are the choices that must be made? Look for the strategic options. Keep a particular eye out for strategies that play out well across multiple scenarios. These are especially attractive for obvious reasons.

- What are the key indicators and navigational beacons that can be used to track reality versus the scenarios that determine where strategy adjustments may be desirable? These are extremely important because they indicate adjustments, and they may indicate when a completely new scenario exercise may be warranted.

Generally, there will be a dedicated team that works on scenario planning in larger companies. However, it is critically important that a broad base of employees be involved in interviews and any other methods available to get their input and expose them to the process and the development of the scenarios. It should be like a platter of ham and eggs being observed by a pig and a chicken. The pig (scenario planning team) is committed. The chicken (the employees being interviewed and such) is involved. Remember the principle benefit of scenario planning is not the scenarios themselves but the impact of the thinking on the culture of the organization: the opening up of your employees' eyes to new thinking.

To further develop the concept of scenario planning, I will share some work I did a few years ago.

***

Unless you have a particular interest in scenario planning, I encourage you to stop reading here and move on to chapter 5.

***

The American University Kogod School of Business was going to offer an emerging-market special course to be taught by multiple professors. I was invited to be one, but—as a nontenured faculty and thus low man on the totem pole—my material couldn't overlap with anybody else's. I got the last pick. Rather than running around and figuring out what eight other professors were going to do, I decided to do something so different it could not possibly overlap with anybody else.

I decided to do a scenario plan around the central question "BRIC: The World Economic and Political Order in 2050." BRIC is the well-known acronym for Brazil, Russia, India, and China. With the support and mental muscle of two of my brightest former students, then alums, I set off to work.

Having covered step 1 of the process (set the central question), the designated stakeholders, given the nature of the course were US multinationals. My helpers would be proxies for their employees. That decided, we set off to work.

Our first work product, looked like figure 9 below. Given our central question, we chose three critical uncertainties: geopolitical power distribution, global economic growth, and degree of economic cooperation. Normally, there are two selected as in diagram 8 above, but—inspired by Royal Dutch Shell's recent work—I chose three. Our axes of uncertainty looked like figure 10 below.

Note the names of the scenarios on diagram 10. There are only three scenarios with this approach rather than four. It may sound simpler, but it's not. For each of the three scenarios, we had to account for the fact that two of the driving forces held sway, but the third one didn't happen. Our scenarios had to account for all three—not two. That was taxing as you will see when I recount the headlines of the scenarios.

Take special note of the names of the scenarios in diagram 10. They are clever and memorable if I do say so myself. Remember, that is part of the guidelines of good scenario planning.

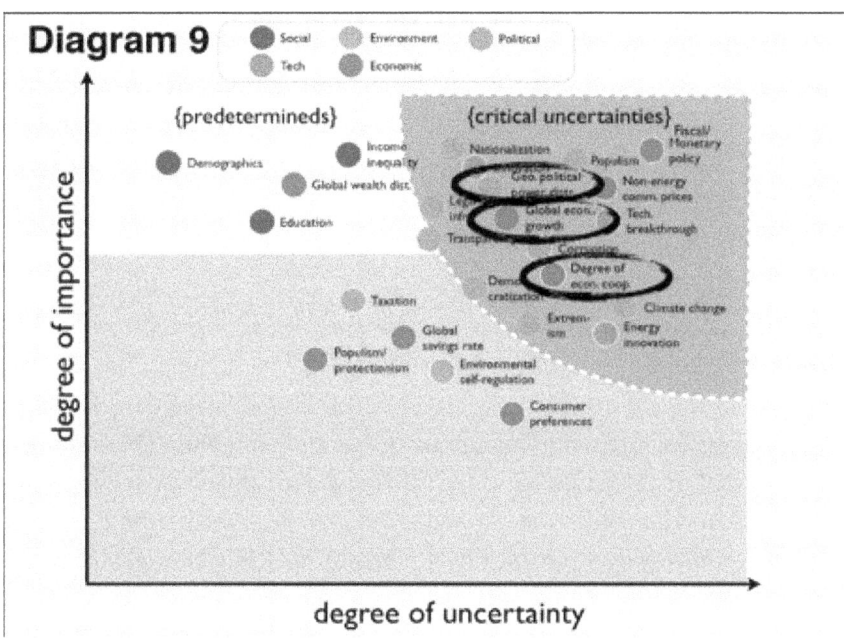

In "Win-Win," as you can imagine, everybody's a winner. Economic prosperity is the order of the day, and a high level of global strategic cooperation makes that happen. In the spirit of Ricardo's comparative advantage, specialization and trade cause economies to boom and prosperity and democracy rule the day. Global GDP growth substantially exceeds that prevailing at the turn of the twenty-first century. Political power plays little role in this scenario. Competition between nation-states is largely of healthy economic competition. The Organization for Economic Cooperation and Development (OECD) countries with BRIC share soft power amicably. The G-20 supplants OECD and BRIC as the dominant forum for meeting and dispute resolution. Robe

The most important venue for dispute resolution becomes the World Trade Organization rather than NATO. Africa rises to become the next set of emerging markets as BRIC approaches OECD levels of GDP per capita (adjusted for purchasing parity). Terrorism abates as the Muslim world reaps the benefits of economic prosperity. How is this utopian world attained? How is it plausible? BRIC countries (particularly China and Russia) behave responsibly as increasing economic and political power inexorably accrues to them and OECD countries accept the inevitable sharing of economic and political power that will come from BRIC's higher economic growth rates. Global strategic cooperation is a major factor facilitating all this, first through growing trade and increasing economic interdependence and secondly in other forums where political power is shared if not amicably then at least through effective negotiation and intermediation.

In "Flip-Flop," strategic cooperation is low. The collapse of the European economy and demise of the euro lead to an unhealthy and ruthless competitive spirit within the global economy. The United States stumbles with virtually flatlined economic growth debilitated by burgeoning debt it depends on China to finance. The situation is worsened by a declining value in the dollar and thus a rising cost of imports. The high cost of social benefits and entitlements in the OECD countries are worn like a shroud. NATO collapses because of spats over money. Nobody wants to pay a fair share of the bills. Global growth rates are low, weighed down by the poor performance of OECD countries, but continue to be healthy in the emerging markets as cheap labor continues to hold sway.

While global strategic cooperation is low, bilateral trade agreements among BRIC countries and Africa ensure their continued growth.

Their economic potential and implied promises of prosperity to their people are met. Terrorism continues to plague the world as Muslims become even more polarized with a growing number of ISIS recruits. Radical Islam cannot find an acceptable place at the global table of economic and political interaction.

As the world fights over a pie that's not growing at an acceptable rate, political power becomes important. Given the relative state of the economies, BRIC assumes a pari passu position with the OECD given the collapse of NATO and the inability of the United States to continue to support its high levels of military spending of bygone years. Much of this dark picture is painted by the OECD's failure to accept the inevitable growth of BRIC and embrace them in their rightful positions of power and prosperity, i.e. we bring it upon ourselves

In "Common Enemy," the darkness of the canvas emanates from BRIC's failure to deliver to their people on both the potential and promise of their economies. As their governments come under tremendous populist pressure, there is a desperate reach for a common enemy to divert dissatisfaction and attention. Here, it would be the OECD that would be positioned as the bad guy responsible for all BRIC's problems. Probably, though not certainly, this strategy would be most intense in China and Russia where totalitarianism or some semblance thereof reigns supreme. While the degree of economic cooperation is high, it manifests itself in some combination of regional and BRIC-centric policies.

No doubt, the reader will have many reactions to the above scenarios—disagreement being among the most prevalent. However, please remember my objective in sharing this work is not to convince you that my depictions of plausible, divergent futures as described for this central question are right. It's more to show you the process and hopefully give you some sense of its value.

Summary

Decision-making is more difficult than gambling.

Gambling is risky. Decision-making is uncertain.

In gambling, probabilities are known or knowable.

In decision-making, probabilities are unknowable.

Good bets have positive expected value, and bad bets have negative expected value.

Good bets can be lost, but they were still good bets.

We have to make assumptions on things we don't know.

Beware the known, it's fraught with potential for biases, suppositions about the unknowable in the present, and presuppositions about the future.

Rules of forecasting:

Forecast often. Eventually you'll be right—remind everyone.

Forecast audaciously and with ambiguity (a way out).

Models can be useful, but limitations need to be respected.

They are abstractions fraught with assumptions (choice of variables).

Computer output precision makes it deceptively believable—beware!

Users of model output don't understand their limitations.

The global financial crisis was a case study of failed financial modeling.

The key variable-omitted banking system—Great Moderation—is a myth.

It assumed rational decision-makers and limited historical data.

Technical sophistication blinded users to its frailty.

Complexity of markets/economies was underestimated.

Hugh Courtney had four levels of uncertainty:

Level 1—uncertainty is limited and forecasting is useful

Level 2—distinct set of outcomes (if/then)

Level 3—bounded range of outcomes

Level 4—not possible to bound a range of outcome—true uncertainty

Nicholas Taleb's black swans are rare occurrence, major

consequences, inevitably clear in hindsight, problem, and underestimate importance.

Dedicate resources to preparation—not prediction.

Forecast from the bottom up and avoid a doctrinaire approach.

Rank assumptions in terms of damage they cause—not plausibility.

Don't trust experts.

Tetlock says an expert's track record equals a dart-throwing chimpanzee.

Experts are massively overconfident. Good predictors are self-critical.

Knowing lots of small things is better than having one single big idea.

Isaiah Berlin showed the hedgehog versus the fox.

Scenario planning is a disciplined process to discuss challenging, plausible divergent futures—not deterministic like a forecast.

Process is more important than the outcome (scenarios themselves).

The impact on the thinking of the participants is important.

A process can develop a scenario plan.

Agree on central question and identify the driving forces.

Select axes of uncertainty—four plausible, divergent scenarios.

Develop key stakeholder implications and navigational beacons.

BRIC: World Economic and Political Order in 2050 has three key drivers:

- BRIC major economic power
- BRIC major political power
- Level of strategic cooperation

Key Scenarios

- "Win-Win"—shared power and global cooperation

- "Flip-Flop"—OECD domination cedes to rising power of BRIC
- "Common Enemy"—BRIC uses to stay in power

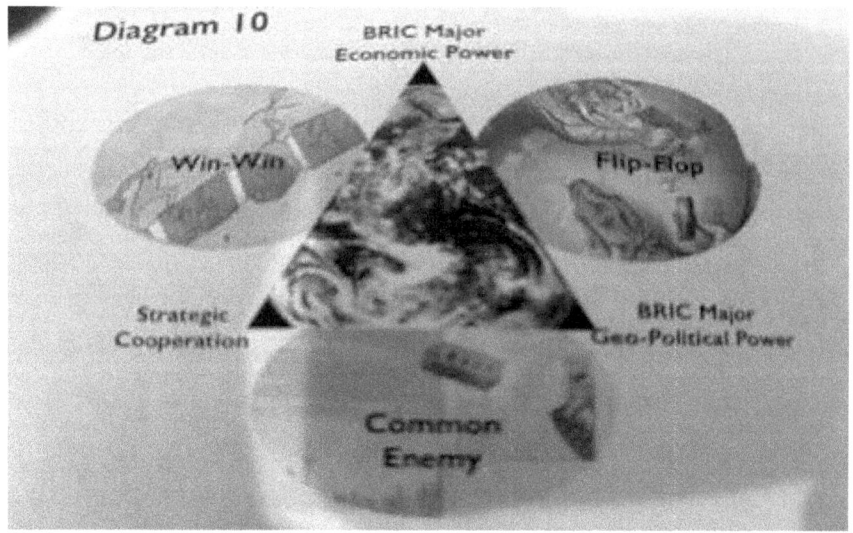

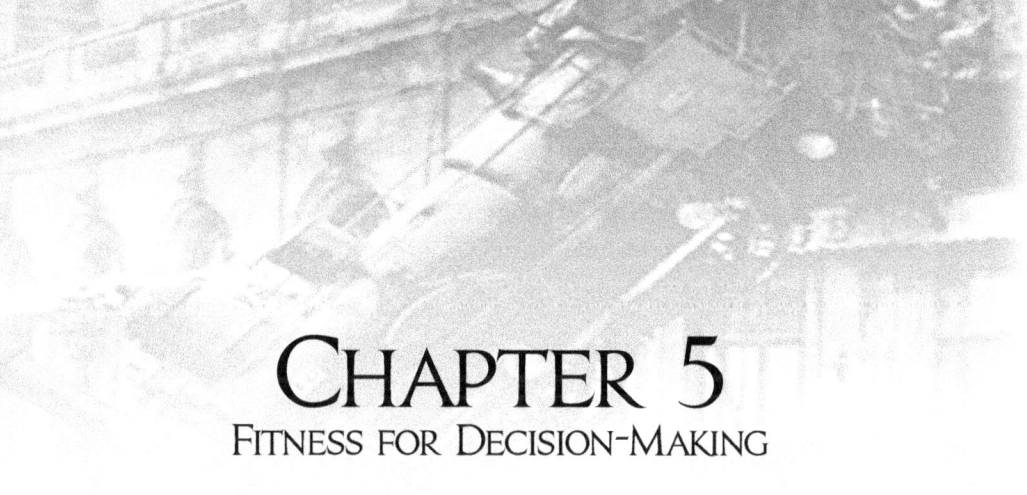

CHAPTER 5
FITNESS FOR DECISION-MAKING

Most U.S. corporations today are over-managed and under-led.[12]
John P. Kotter

Process, Process, Process. It's all about process!

"Many leaders fail because they think of decisions as events, not processes."[13] In chapter 2, I posited on McKinsey's point that process trumps analytics in decision-making by a factor of six to one. The logic supporting this is simple. Strong process will ferret out weak analytics, but the inverse is not the case. How do we ensure that our process is strong? We apply the attributes related to leadership, management, and oversight as described below. That will dramatically reduce the probability of failure. It will help make us far more rational than otherwise, help us avoid confusing the complex with the complicated, and help cope with black swans and other issues related to uncertainty.

I have already covered various tips on avoiding traps for all three of the drivers of failure. This chapter explores the skills it takes to apply these tips and further reduce the odds of failure. It is built around three skills sets I characterize as leadership, management, and oversight.

---

12. *What Leaders Really Do,* John P. Kotter, *Harvard Business Review*, December 2001.
13. *The Art of Critical Decision-Making*, Michael A. Roberto, The Great Courses.

The focus is on maximizing rationality and effectively coping with complexity and uncertainty.

So, are we fit in these three areas? Are our skill levels in each up to the task of making the decision at hand? As in other chapters, while the focus is on decision-making in business, the concepts apply in personal decision-making too. Where necessary, I will make that distinction.

First let's deal with leadership and management. John P. Kotter developed important distinctions between leadership and management in his seminal work, *What Leaders Really Do*. He also expressed a strong view indicated in the above quote. I will draw on that work extensively because I feel it is spot-on. Also, as always, it's important that we have a shared vocabulary.

What follows is a discussion of what leaders and managers do. The emphasis is on *do*. Leadership is as leadership does. Management is as management does. They are activities by definition. In my definitions, we need both leadership and management skills in varying degrees for sound decision-making. The distinction comes from the nature of the jobs we are in or the situations we face. Fundamentally, the more complexity in the situation we face, the more leadership is required and the less management is required. The more uncertainty we face, the more leadership skills and the less management skills are required in confronting the situation. This holds for decision-making in both professional and personal situations.

Leadership versus Management

Management is about arranging and telling. Leadership is about nurturing and enhancing.

—*Tom Peters*

In writing about leadership, I must start with the words of Nelson Mandela:

> I always remember the axiom; a leader … is like a shepherd. He stays behind the flock, letting the most nimble go out ahead, whereupon the others follow, not realizing that all along they are being directed from behind.

These simple words capture the essence of what the following few pages are all about.

Leadership must determine the purpose of the company. Max De Pree said, "The first responsibility of a leader is to define reality." Why does the company exist? In the case of American Express, I would suggest its purpose is to provide the world's consumers with financial services. Citigroup has a similar purpose in my view—but with a broader client base that includes corporations.

A year ago, I became involved in a start-up, Big Word Club, that provides educational entertainment to kids by building vocabulary in fast, fun, and effective ways because "knowing more words makes you smarter." Our purpose is to give kids the opportunity to have fun while learning to fall in love with words. Such is the nature of purpose statements. They provide context and guidance in decision-making.

We, as individuals, utilize our personal leadership skills to determine our purpose as well, just as company leadership does. In a sense, our purpose is an expression of our higher self. Why are we here? Besides procreation, why do we exist? Our purpose is a matter of personal choice (independent agents acting in parallel). "Why do I exist?" Each of us creates our own response(s) to that question. That response is our beacon, our guide in decision-making.

In conjunction with articulating the purpose, leadership skills determine the vision for the firm. What does the company want to become? The same is true for us as individuals. In thinking about vision, I always reach back to my days at American Express where considerable time and money were spent in the early nineties on developing a vision statement. The result was the following: "To become the world's most respected service brand." I thought it was brilliant, and I still do. I don't know how much it cost, but, whatever it was, it was worth it. In part, its brilliance lies in its elegant simplicity, yet it says so much. It is highly aspirational, and many employees would find it inspirational.

It is noteworthy that there is nothing about charge or credit cards, traveler's checks, or even travel itself in the statement, even though these all are integral parts of what the company does today. It doesn't even have some form of the word finance in it even though the company today is essentially a financial institution. These are all part of the company's mission, i.e. what the company does today. As previously mentioned, vision is aspirational. At the time, CEO Harvey Golub said that a vision statement should have the verb "to become" in it.

Citibank didn't have a vision statement to my knowledge, but if it did, it would have been something like becoming the leading global provider of financial services. Today, Citibank's vision (now known as Citigroup) seems to be narrowing and is more elusive, at least for me.

My start-up would like to become the global leader in helping all kids fall in love with words. It wants to bridge the *word gap* by providing digital and print content that builds vocabulary for preschoolers through fifth grade of all socioeconomic levels.

The mission of the firm explains what it does on a day-to-day basis. I don't remember the American Express mission statement back then, but I'm confident it was built around charge and credit cards, traveler's checks, travel, and premier service quality. Since mission is about today, it would have been built around the products and services offered at that time. I don't recall Citibank's either, but it would have logically been built around something like being a leading provider of financial services to the world. My start-up's mission is to bring schoolteachers, parents, and kids together for shared vocabulary-learning experiences through digital media delivered on mobile apps and companion books. It's a bit of a mouthful and may mean we're trying to do too much for a start-up, but we plan on a phased rollout.

In terms of the linkage in this regard between leadership and management, I am reminded of a Japanese proverb: "Vision without action is a daydream. Action without vision is a nightmare." Leadership is the vision, and management is the action. However, management acting without the context established by leadership (purpose, vision, and mission) is indeed a nightmare. Management is all about execution. Thomas Edison said, "Vision without execution is hallucination." Again, they are opposite sides of the same coin.

Leadership also asks questions—particularly *why*. Management has a lot to do with the answers, particularly by saying, "here's how." So, they are joined at the hip. I think Max De Pree got it right when he wrote, "What we do is always going to be a consequence of who it is we intend to become." We are, after all, the sum of the decisions we make.

Another key thought on the distinction between leadership and management is that leadership is all about effectiveness (doing the right thing). Management is all about efficiency (doing things right). De Pree also said, "Leaders can delegate efficiency, but they must deal personally with effectiveness."[14]

In conjunction with the above, leadership needs to determine what the company's culture should be: what behavioral norms and values will best serve the company in fulfilling its purpose, performing its mission, and moving toward its vision. Management is responsible for living the culture and ensuring that the culture is baked into the company's day-to-day operations.

At American Express, I found the culture to be gentlemanly, but the politics were vicious. At Citibank, we competed with each other and felt we had no external competition. It was arrogance personified. It was the star system. Teamwork wasn't valued that much in the late eighties and early nineties. You ate what you killed. Carl Icahn said, "If you want a friend, buy a dog." That was a long time ago. Hopefully both cultures have changed for the better.

I believe in the power of teams (complex adaptive systems). I think they are the key part of a winning culture in most circumstances today. Leadership should set performance goals that only can be reached by high-performance teams. Management, to be successful, must live in a culture where teamwork, not bureaucracy, is a core part of the culture. Team decision-making is tough. It consumes significant energy and time, but in the end, you will most often get a better result than with individual effort. So, the extra time and effort are worth it. Teams are also more nimble than rigid hierarchical structures. They also generally produce greater innovation.

Culture, of course, also needs to be about performance. Jack Welch, retired CEO of General Electric, established a practice at GE of weeding out the bottom 10 percent. In an annual report, Welch wrote, "Not removing [the] bottom 10 percent early in their careers is not only a management failure, but … a form of cruelty." So, Welch views this as a constantly evolving process of hiring and developing talent while constantly sorting out recruiting and training/

---

14. *Leadership is an Art*, Max de Pree.

development failures. No recruiting and training/development process is perfect. Recognizing this, Welch says you need an ongoing process of terminating your recruiting and training/development mistakes. The alternative is to have them suffer the "cruelty" of living in a high-performance environment where they just do not measure up.

Leadership focuses on strategy while management focuses on tactics. Leadership is concerned with industry trends, disruptive technologies, and black swans. These are complex situations and occasionally chaotic ones and thus present opaque or wicked problems.

Management is concerned with this month's production, sales levels, organizational structure, staff selection and performance, controlling costs, and providing day-to-day direction to the organization. These are complicated situations with transparent though often difficult problems and decisions. Both strategy and tactics are important, and attention must be paid to each. But as tasks, strategy and tactics are different.

Put simply, management skills ensure the right decisions are made to keep the trains running on time. Leadership skills ensure an optimal decision is made in the determination of where the next rail line should be built. That's because, on the complexity spectrum, as previously mentioned, management deals with the simple and the complicated situations while leadership deals with complex and, at times, chaotic situations. Consequently, the problems management faces are transparent while leadership faces opaque problems and often *wicked* problems.

That doesn't mean that management is somehow easy. Complicated situations with transparent problems (everything is known or knowable) can be, and often are, very

difficult. Sound management requires great discipline and both right- and left-brain intellect. Its importance must be recognized and respected in any organization. Kotter is correct about most companies being overmanaged and under-led, but he is quick to point out that undermanaging a situation can readily lead to chaos (see Enron in chapter 6).

Leadership is required in situations where innovation is needed. It is all about innovation and *design thinking*, a methodology used to solve opaque/wicked problems. Management and its related bureaucracy tend to stifle innovation and creativity. Management wants compliance rather than innovation. While management is all about stability, leadership is about change.

Leadership and management also have a different longitudinal dimension. Leadership is focused on the future. "What might the long term bring?" Management is focused on today, this month, this quarter, and this year. It focuses on budgeting and forecasting, performing operational reviews, and analyzing variances by comparing actual performance with budget and forecast. Leadership is focused on scenario planning and related big-picture issues. Consequently, leadership operates at higher levels of uncertainty. A great way to think about this is that Martin Luther King, one of our greatest American leaders, didn't say, "I have a plan." That's what a manager would have said. Instead, he said, "I have a dream." That's how a real leader thinks. And with complex and wicked problems, solutions tend to come as dreams and not plans. Max De Pree said, "The signs of outstanding leadership appear primarily among the followers."

Another important characteristic of leaders is embodied in the following statement in the foreword to Max De Pree's cited book by James O'Toole, from the University of Southern California's Graduate School of Business: "Leaders will have the self-confidence, as Max says, to 'encourage contrary opinions' and 'to abandon themselves to the strengths of others.' In short, the true leader is a listener."

As you move up the ladder of the organization and/or decisions become of greater importance and complexity, the balance between management and leadership shifts. Making the numbers is still necessary, but it is not sufficient. More and more time and attention needs to be paid to leadership activities and less—though still some—to management. So, the picture is like diagram 5 but with "Engineering/Art" now labeled "Management/Leadership." Diagram 11 below shows that, with increased complexity, more leadership and less management is required.

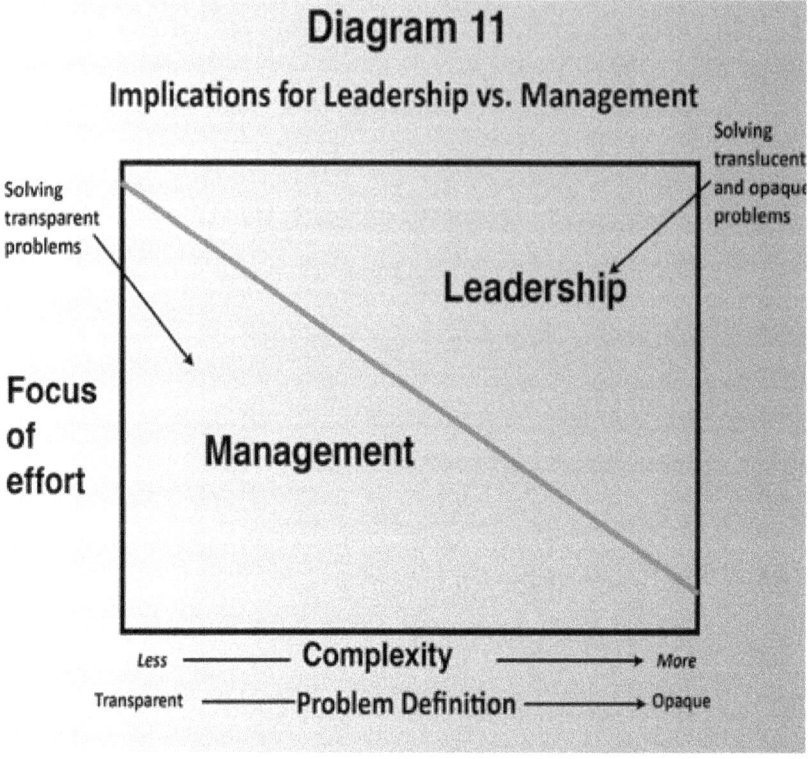

Note that leadership equates to design. Really, more directly, it equates to art. Management, on the other hand, equates to engineering and science.

While leadership and management are distinctly different activities, as individuals, we must be able to lead *and* manage in order to be successful decision-makers. Being one-dimensional is problematic. Having said that, recognizing our limitations is important. That's why CEOs (mostly practicing leadership) so often pair up with COOs (mostly practicing management). Then, depending on the situation and the kind of problem one is trying to solve (refer to chapter 3), one of the two skill sets is required.

In simple and complicated situations that pose transparent problems, management skills are required to make sound decisions. In complex or chaotic situations, leadership skills are required to make the right decisions in order to solve the translucent and wicked problems that accompany them.

Overmanaged and Under-Led: A Case Study

Bureaucracy is the death of all sound work.
—Albert Einstein

All too often, great managers lack the core qualities of leadership. They are all about management but have no sense of leadership or of the ramifications of their tough-minded management style on their respective organizations. Here's an example of what can happen in an overmanaged organization.

I was the CFO of a large, highly profitable group of related businesses for a few years that was heavy on management and light on leadership. It was functionally organized and more *siloed* than would normally be considered healthy. The area of the organization where over-management principally manifested itself was in the operating side of the business: the data centers, processing units, and call centers. The head of back-office operations and technology (I'll call him Steve) was a really strong manager. He was scary strong and ran a tight ship, but almost all of the qualities of leadership previously mentioned were sorely lacking. Disagreement was not welcome and generally punished if it occurred. Innovation fell by the wayside because, at least in part, there was no risk-taking. Fear of failure, as already discussed, is worse than failure because it leads to not trying. That was the case here.

Given the nature of the operations-oriented activities, strong process management was more than appropriate. It was necessary. Management for compliance rather than leading innovation was in order. However, taken to excess as it was, with no countervailing force of leadership, the organization became dysfunctional. Not only does innovation and risk-taking suffer, bad news tends not to flow upward because people don't want to hear it. It gets suppressed until a blowup occurs. The following is just one example.

Besides operational responsibility, Steve also had revenue responsibility for the very operations-oriented business. It made sense that it would fall under his wing. One day, the CFO (I'll call him Dan) stopped by my office and made a comment about monthly earnings that confused me. I couldn't understand the significance of what he was saying, and I pressed him for details. The story started to come out. The business had been missing budgeted financial targets for net income systematically for a few years. The bad news had been hidden by under-accruing expense and over-accruing revenue, thus artificially inflating income. This overstated the business's financial performance to make it look like it was meeting its financial targets when in fact it was not. Their plan was to "catch up" when the business results ran better than budget, but it just didn't happen. In fact, the hole kept getting deeper—until it was too big to hide.

Of course, this breaks the rules of sound accounting and financial control and is a breach of common sense and ethics. It happened before Sarbanes-Oxley[15] legislation was passed. Otherwise, the CFO of the business and his boss, the business manager, would likely have ended up in jail. And since sign-offs move up the chain of command, yours truly might have been there right along with them. As it was, they both got fired. The organization ended up writing off $20 million. But the core problem, an organization run with an iron fist that suppressed bad news out of fear of reprisal, was never addressed. Why not? Because nobody wanted to deal with the issue. Steve was a very powerful and otherwise successful senior manager. This was clearly an exemplar of the opening Kotter quote on being overmanaged and under-led.

Leadership Can Have a Short Fuse

In the past two decades, 30 percent of Fortune 500 CEOs have lasted less than three years.[16] Because leadership operates in complex situations and in high levels of uncertainty, the propensity to fail is higher than with management challenges. One just has to look at the rising rate of failure of CEOs over the past twenty years as noted in the quote above. I submit this is the result of the rising level of complexity and uncertainty (refer to chapters 3 and 4).

Booz Allen Hamilton reports that the global average time in position is now just 7.6 years, down from 9.5 years in 1995. The Center for Creative Leadership has pointed out that two out of every five new

---

15. Sarbanes-Oxley Act Section 404 mandates that all publicly traded companies must establish internal controls and procedures for financial reporting amongst other things.
16. "Why Lonely Leaders Are Bad for Business," Ray Williams, *Psychology Today*.

CEOs fail in the first eighteen months, which Dan Ciampa cites in his article "Almost Ready: How Leaders Move Up." Further, Ciampa points out that when a company reaches outside for a designated CEO successor, "only one-quarter of these candidates were successful at either being named CEO or at staying in the CEO job for more than two years."

Comparing and Contrasting
Leadership and Management—Case Studies

Management is doing things right; leadership is doing the right things.

—*Peter Drucker*

One of my favorite examples of a great leader and a great manager is President John Fitzgerald Kennedy. He was a man of great vision and remarkable skills in expressing that vision. As just one example, take this excerpt from his inaugural address of January 20, 1961:

> And so, my fellow Americans: ask not what your country can do for you — ask what you can do for your country. My fellow citizens of the world: ask not what America will do for you, but what together we can do for the freedom of man.

Many consider Kennedy a man of great words but few deeds. He is thought of as a great leader but weak at managing legislation through Congress. Nothing could be further from the truth. Larry O'Brien said, "A myth had arisen that he [Kennedy] was uninterested in Congress, or that he 'failed' with Congress. The facts, I believe, are otherwise. Kennedy's legislative record in 1961–63 was the best of any president since Roosevelt's first term." That's quite a management track record.

Another example of a great leader/manager in a whole different realm is Diane von Furstenberg. She came to New York City as a "young princess" in her own words, married to Prince Egon of Furstenberg. Ms. von Furstenberg is the daughter of an Auschwitz Holocaust survivor. She credits her mother with her learning that "fear is not an option," an exemplary characteristic of a leader. Her iconic wrap dress is still being worn today by women around the world, decades after its introduction. She said, "My favorite days are the ones where I deal only with my own team, design, marketing, working on the next accessories' collection." For me, the emphasis is on the word *team*. She doesn't take sole credit for her world-class designs for the "working girl." While a more creative genius than most leaders, she embodies the core qualities of leadership and management. In an interview with Fareed Zakaria of CNN, she said "You have to be serious and work hard. Reality has its ups and its downs." These are exemplary statements of a real manager.

Yet another example of a great leader/manager is Ursula Burns, former CEO of Xerox. Ms. Burns graduated as a mechanical engineer when Xerox was the leader in the photocopying market. Yes, contrary to the earlier examples given, engineers can be great leaders. Ms. Burns states:

> As I've progressed in my career, I've come to appreciate — and really value — the other attributes that define a company's success beyond the P&L: great leadership, long-term financial strength, ethical business practices, evolving business strategies, sound governance, powerful brands, values-based decision-making.

This is the statement of a leader/manager. As an indication of her full leadership capability, Ms. Burns was also quoted as saying on the same website:

> We all need to be more impatient with the status quo. I believe we all need to shift the emphasis in our thinking ... from why we can't create more jobs to how we can create more jobs ... from why we can't compete to how we can compete ... from why hunger and poverty and injustice exist in the world to how they can be eliminated ... In other words, we all need to be a little more impatient.

That's the statement of a real leader.

Sometimes it takes two to tango. Leadership and management often come in a CEO/COO team. When I was a shavetail at Citibank, I had the privilege of spending time with then chairman Walter Wriston. Walt was one of the finest bankers of the twentieth century and a real gentleman. One day, we flew on the corporate jet to Detroit with my boss Allyn Gallup to call on one of my customers, Burroughs

Corporation (now Unisys).

I don't remember anything of the company visit, but I vividly recall the conversation during the plane ride. Walt regaled us with story after story. The one I most remember was about his working relationship with Bill Spencer, then president of the bank. Walt called him Billy. Likely he was the only one in the bank who did. He let Billy run the place, and when Walt traveled, he never worried about the "shop" because Billy was there covering for him. The fact is Billy kept the trains running on time while Walt decided where the next rail line should be built. Together, they had leadership and management covered beautifully.

Another dynamic duo is Mark Zuckerberg and Sheryl Sandberg. Zuckerberg and the Facebook board recognized the need for strong management talent to scale Facebook. It was a task beyond Zuckerberg. He needed help. Reaching out to Sandberg was a brilliant move.

In fact, it has been said of Facebook that Zuckerberg provides the imagination, while Sheryl Sandberg, Facebook's chief operating officer, provides the execution around his vision. Her experience at Google as vice president of global online sales and operations prepared her well for the task. As importantly, Zuckerberg and Sandberg share the same values, complementary strengths, commitment, mutual trust and the mutual respect needed to continue to drive the company forward.

This chapter started with a quote from John Kotter: "Most US corporations today are overmanaged and under-led." I would submit a classic example of this is Mike Lazaridis, founder of Research in Motion (now called Blackberry). Lazaridis, a scientist by inclination (according to Wikipedia, "he won a prize at the Windsor Public Library for reading every science book in the library") and an engineer by educational background (according to Wikipedia, he quit two months before graduation), came up with a brilliant invention: the wireless mobile device called the Blackberry. It was so good, in fact, that it enjoyed a meteoric rise in market share to an apex of around 20 percent in 2009–2010 and was even nicknamed the Crackberry because it was so addictive.

Lazaridis was enamored with the science of the device—and not the marketplace. He didn't see it coming when Apple went after the top of the market with a "cooler" product. Then Android software from Google armed all the non-premium smartphone providers with devices matching or surpassing Blackberry's functionality at substantially reduced prices. It has been in the going-out-of-business business ever since with a drop in stock price from over $200 per share to around $10 at midyear 2017. It has gone from being the dominant player in the global smartphone market (20 percent market share in 2009) to 0.2 percent share in the second quarter of 2014.

Another example of a company being overmanaged and under-led is Microsoft under the stewardship of CEO Steve Ballmer. Ballmer was handpicked by founder Bill Gates, his college roommate. Some have characterized this as the luckiest draw of a roommate in history. Ballmer achieved a perfect score of eight hundred in his math SAT and was a National Merit Scholar. He graduated magna cum laude from Harvard with degrees in mathematics and economics. Unfortunately, while he was a successful chief operating officer and manager under the leadership of Gates, I believe he failed miserably in transitioning to CEO and leader.

Over the twelve years of his stewardship, he siloed and bureaucratized the organization, destroying its innovative instincts. Its biggest innovation during his tenure was the Xbox, small fish for an organization with such potential. He also led the company to its first quarterly loss. Its cultural capacity for innovation was weak. Its Surface Pro 3 lagged well behind the Kindle Fire and the iPad. Although its Windows model smartphone got good reviews, it held a mere 5 percent of the smartphone market, likely due to its late market entry and high cost. Ballmer's swan song, the purchase of Nokia, is yet another example of an acquisition where $1 + 1 = 1\frac{1}{2}$. Microsoft ended up writing off nearly the entire $7.9 billion it paid. Since when does the merger of two weak players in a market make a strong player?

Ballmer's successor, Satya Nadella, has had his hands full. So far, he has shown himself to be the sorely needed leader of cultural change. The company's position in cloud computing is strong and trending upward. His recent purchase of LinkedIn may be a further step in the right direction, particularly since CEO Jeff Weiner will stay on and founder Reid Hoffman will go on the Microsoft board.

Interestingly, Nadella defies gravity as an insider coming from a weak culture sorely in need of change, which is generally not a recipe for success. Yet he appears to be driving the cultural change needed to restore innovation. Today, Microsoft's financial strength is unquestioned as it successfully maintained its AAA bond rating in the $20 billion bond issuance to finance the LinkedIn purchase.

So, what happens when an organization is undermanaged and over-led. Chaos ensues. George Shaheen, CEO of now-defunct online grocer Webvan is a prime example. The Webvan saga occurred at the height of the dot-com bubble at the turn of the millennium. Shaheen, who had been the president of Anderson Consulting from 1989 through 1999, took over Webvan with a vision of changing the way that groceries were purchased. Just use the internet to place your order, and it comes to your door. It was that elegantly simple, but it didn't work in part because it was an idea ahead of its time. Also, Shaheen executed with an irrational bias of overconfidence.

Shaheen was a leader with no discernible management skills. He drove the business model across the country without validated learning that the business model would work in its first market. That's financial suicide. The numbers were staggering and an example of how awry things can get in a financial bubble. Webvan managed an IPO raising $375 million that gave the company a valuation of $4.8 billion. At the time of the offering, the company had cumulative revenue of $395,000 and losses of $50 million. It is stounding in hindsight.

Shaheen and his team—none of whom had any experience in the supermarket industry—burned through about $400 million in capital, cheered on by their feckless investors to cries of "first-mover advantage." A good manager would have had the discipline to know what she/he didn't know and would have tried to learn it first—in a disciplined trial-and-error way

If Shaheen had pivoted away from what didn't work and toward what worked, he likely would have learned that the idea was flawed in the first market. Even if he took it to a second market to pivot away from things that didn't work in the first to try more new things, eventually he would have learned. With this approach, he would have likely saved the investors hundreds of millions of dollars. Instead, Shaheen and his colleagues covered ten cities on their way to twenty-six before they ran out of money. Webvan has been billed by some as the largest dot-com failure ahead of Pets.com.

Oversight

Governance and leadership are the yin and the yang of successful organizations. If you have leadership without governance you risk tyranny, fraud, and personal fiefdoms. If you have governance without leadership you risk atrophy, bureaucracy, and indifference.

—*Mark Goyder, founder of Tomorrow's Company*

Why are there brakes on a car? So, the car can go faster. Think about it. How slow would you have to go if your car had weak brakes or no brakes at all? Not very fast at all. Have you ever checked out the brakes on high-performance cars? They have massive disks and calipers, often with ceramic brake pads (heat dissipation). Why? Because in racing, the driver who brakes the latest (and hardest) going into a turn without losing control will generally maintain the highest speed (all else being equal). That's a key tactic in winning races. That kind of hard braking requires large surface area disks and various sophisticated braking-system characteristics to prevent fading or loss of braking efficiency due to overheating. Thus, great brakes enable high-speed driving.

Car brakes serve as a metaphor for controlling rapid change. If we reach back to what decision-making is all about—bringing a situation from its current state to some desired state—the faster we want to do that, the greater our need for oversight (brakes). That is not to say that oversight isn't helpful in almost all decisions. It simply says that, with good oversight, you can safely move the process along faster—from problem identification to decision-making through to execution.

Here is an important clarification. I use the term *oversight* as meaning the function of watching or guiding for the sake of proper direction. It is not used to imply control, though it might in some cases (as noted below). It is also not limited to the boardroom.

Most frequently, decision-making oversight comes from mentors and bosses. Depending on the level of the decision-maker, it can come from the board of directors or shareholders. Also, depending on the nature and size of the business, it can come from regulators and legislators. Let's cover mentors first.

First, let's get on the same page with our terminology. I'll go with Wiki's definition of mentorship.

> Mentorship is a relationship in which a more experienced or more knowledgeable person helps guide a less experienced or less knowledgeable person. The mentor may be older or younger than the person being mentored, but she or he must have a certain area of expertise. It is a learning and development partnership between someone with vast experience and someone who wants to learn.

Neville D. Christie is an executive coach whose work on the subject has been particularly informative:

> Research on why people have become masterful in a niche – professions, trades, sports, science, and the arts, highlights the importance of having mentors. Talk to any great software engineer, project manager, athlete or artist and they will tell you that their mentor(s) made the difference. We've all heard the quote "great scientists stand on the shoulders of those who preceded them." Mentor/protégé relationships were the earliest forms of learning and professional development. Today having multiple mentors is a necessity because so much is changing around us. No one person can coach others in all the domains of a complex workplace.

Mentorship is accessible from many sources, but a good mentor is hard to find. A smart mentee treats them right when they find one. The relationship needs to be nurtured over time, and the more invested in the relationship, the greater the return—on both sides.

The flow of assistance from a good mentor to their mentee is both bountiful and varied. The various aspects of mentorship include providing direction, coaching, motivation, advice, support, training, and ultimately being a role model. Being a mentor in also highly rewarding. My teaching position at the American University Kogod

School of Business (Kogod) has afforded me many opportunities to assume such a role during the fifteen years I've been in the classroom. It is one of the reasons I teach. When students reach back and, in so doing, reach out, it gives a unique, warm feeling. If you, the reader, are inclined to teach someday, I heartily recommend it.

The value of mentorship is both intuitive and well documented. Intuitively, we all know the value of seeking out wisdom. And mentorship generally is the quest for access to greater experiences than our own. Therefore, we are seeking access to a higher level of *computational intelligence*, which we discussed in chapter 2 when we covered *bounded rationality*. Oversight in mentorship is more than that. First and foremost, it is a powerful weapon in the battle against irrationality. However, it is also invaluable in coping with complexity and uncertainty.

In business decision-making, oversight comes in many forms as well. Some are helpful, and others are not so helpful. In mentorship, you get to choose your mentor. It's actually a mutual selection process. That is often not the case in the business world. Boards of directors and bosses provide oversight, and the choice is limited to your choice of where you work.

So, oversight also comes from the boss. Everybody has one, including CEOs. They answer to the board of directors. The board of directors and the CEO answer to the firms' stakeholders (shareholders, analysts, employees, communities, regulators, clients, and suppliers). And each of the stakeholders answers to its own constituencies.

Corporate governance has become all the rage, particularly following the global financial crisis—and for good reason. A strong board can do remarkably positive things for a company, and a weak board can do terribly bad things to a company. One of the principal roles of a board of directors is to plan and ensure execution of a robust CEO-succession strategy. Put more abruptly, the board is responsible for hiring and firing the CEO. Yet surveys show the results are poor in both these areas. CEOs have been failing at a startlingly high rate, and that rate has been increasing over time. Some experts argue (see below) that the problem is the selection process or the grooming process (of internal candidates). Further, there are a plethora of examples of highly questionable firings (discussed later in this chapter).

Nonetheless, while directors describe CEO succession as one of their most important issues, they hardly seem consumed by it. In a survey by Mercer Delta and the University of Southern California, 40 percent of corporate directors called their involvement in CEO-succession planning less than optimal. (I would hazard to guess that far fewer are satisfied with the outcome of their involvement.) Only 21 percent responded that they were satisfied with their level of participation in developing internal candidates for senior management.

A packed agenda seems one of the culprits. Governance and fiduciary duties, in particular, command an outsized share of boards' attention. Mercer Delta asked directors to compare the amount of time they spend now with the amount they spent a year earlier on nine key activities. Large majorities reported devoting more or many more hours to monitoring accounting, Sarbanes-Oxley, risk, and financial performance. They also reported spending less time interacting with and preparing potential CEO successors than on any other activity. Yet boards' work on succession represents a substantial amount of the value they deliver. If the choice of CEO successor is truly outstanding, all subsequent decisions become easier.

Yet almost half of companies with revenue greater than $500 million have no meaningful CEO-succession plan, according to the National Association of Corporate Directors. Even those that have plans aren't happy with them. The Corporate Leadership Council (CLC), a human-resource research organization, surveyed 276 large companies in 2015 and found that only 20 percent of responding HR executives was satisfied with their top-management succession processes.

The track record for the selection of outside CEOs is worse than that of insiders. In North America, 55 percent of outside CEOs who departed in 2003 were forced to resign by their boards, compared with 34 percent of insiders, Booz Allen reports. In Europe, 70 percent of departing outsiders got the boot, compared with 55 percent of insiders. Some outside CEOs are barely around long enough to see their photographs hung in the headquarters lobby.

Oversight Run Amuck—Some Case Studies

Psychological pathologies among infamous past boards of General Motors, American Express, Gap, Jet Blue, Apple, Hewlett Packard, and Motorola may offer insight.[17]

—Jeffrey Sonnenfeld

Clearly Sonnenfeld has a view on boards and their decisions. I won't run through all his examples, but I will highlight those that I feel are the most egregious. The sordid tale of HP (previously Hewlett-Packard) is a great place to begin. Its failed succession planning goes all the way back to the selection of Carly Fiorina in 1999 as an outsider replacing CEO and insider Lew Platt (CEO from 1992 until 1999). He was a career HP executive. It is remarkable that Carly was in the job for a month before the board even met her. The same was true for a later CEO, Leo Apothaker.

Carly's appointment was the first time in the company's history when the board reached for an outsider to run the then thirteenth-place Fortune 500 company. Choosing Carly was a big bet by the board. While she had been a successful executive at Lucent, she had never run a publicly held company or led anything close to the size and complexity (yes, complexity) of HP. She was hired to lead cultural change, previously described herein as one of the toughest challenges faced by a leader.

She started off her time at the helm by successfully winning a bitter shareholder fight over the acquisition of Compaq with the opposition led by none other than David Hewlett himself. Go, Carly!

Unfortunately, she failed to effectively lead HP through the desperately needed cultural change to make it less an engineering and product company to be more a market-oriented company. Carly was fired five years later, but the board didn't stop there. They proceeded to parade outside CEO after outside CEO (Mark Hurd, Leo Apothaker, and now Meg Whitman) through the company. From Carly in 1999 to Meg in 2011, that's four CEOs in twelve years—and that excludes two interim CEOs. Meanwhile, HP stock has dropped from its peak of

17. "Another suicidal board? How DuPont's directors failed Ellen Kullman," Jeffrey Sonnenfeld, Senior Associate Dean of Executive Programs, Yale School of Management, *Fortune*, October 13, 2015.

$76.50/share in 2000 to $18.50 in mid-2017.

Here are some other examples. Gil Amelio left Apple 17 months after he arrived from National Semiconductor. Ex-IBMer Richard Thoman was out of the top spot at Xerox after thirteen months. David Siegel gave up the wheel at Avis Rent a Car for US Airways, but he departed two years later. Ron Johnson was fired as CEO of JC Penney after a scant seventeen months in the position. He left a path of destruction in his wake as measured by a decline of same-store sales (the basic metric of retail) of 32 percent in less than a year.

In the case of the DuPont board's dismissal of Ellen Kullman in 2015, it clearly appeared to outside observer Jeffrey Sonnenfeld that this was more a case of groupthink than shortcomings in Kullman's performance. His cited article throws this dismissal in the hopper with Carly among many others, including one at American Express that I saw up close and personal.

It occurred not long after I joined the company and while I was still CFO of American Express Bank Ltd. (before I became president). James ("Jim") D. Robinson III was summarily dismissed by the board in a veritable coup engineered by Rawleigh Warner, former chairman of Mobil Corp. in collaboration with Howard Clark Sr., previously CEO of AmEx who, ironically, had handpicked Robinson as his successor. Jim had brilliantly led American Express's direct marketing revolution, marrying technology and customer segmentation.

Being two levels down from Jim, I didn't know him well, but I will say that he went out of his way to personally welcome me to the company when I joined in 1992, and he took an interest in my work afterward. He was a real gentleman who made you feel like you were the only person in the room when he talked to you. Having said that, Jim had made a series of strategic decisions (mostly acquisitions) over many years that created results in which Rawleigh and Howard decided they could not abide. So, they huddled and set in motion a successful plan to oust Jim. According to Jeffrey Sonnenfeld, "They expressed their frustration with briefly declining stock prices at AmEx. Ultimately, the week of governance turmoil cost the company an additional 9.3 percent of stock value." It was indeed a complex (not complicated) situation.

The following is a great example of a failed CEO selection from another of my alma maters: Citigroup. It was their board's selection of Chuck Prince as CEO. I wrote about this in an earlier chapter, but it's worth repeating in this context. Chuck is an attorney who had been Sandy Weil's (the then CEO) "deals guy." As I mentioned earlier, he had never led or managed much prior to finding himself on the throne of Citigroup. He had limited experience with regulated companies. While he did have a brief stint as chief operating officer of Citigroup, he was not a banker. And now he was the CEO of one of the largest banks in the world. What were Sandy and the board thinking? Sandy had clearly mesmerized the board. And they were not a group of lightweights. Here are the names of just a few of its members at that time—any one (or all) of whom should have known better:

Robert E. Rubin, seventieth Secretary of Treasury, member of the board and cochairman of Goldman Sachs

- Richard A. Parsons, chairman and CEO of Time Warner
- Alain J. P. Belda, chairman of the board and CEO of Alcoa
- Anne M. Mulcahy, chairwoman of the board and CEO of Xerox
- Roberto Hernandez, chairman of the board and former CEO of Banco Nacional de Mexico, the second-largest bank in Mexico (acquired by Citigroup in 2002)
- Kenneth T. Derr, former CEO of Chevron
- Judith Rodin, president of the Rockefeller Foundation and previously president of the University of Pennsylvania and provost of Yale University

One can conclude from this list that the problem is not insufficient qualifications. Of course, there are some examples on the good side. General Electric is perhaps at the top of the list. General Electric CEOs have been all internal throughout its long history. And it has also been known for its legendary CEOs. Jack Welch, thought by many to have been the top performing CEO of the twentieth century, is perhaps the highest-profile example. But even more important than producing a Jack Welch is the track record of always having a great internal candidate as CEO. This includes Jack's successor, Jeff Immelt, as well as Jeff's successor, John Flannery. Unfortunately, the GE example is rare.

There are also examples of boards doing the right thing in troubled times. One is the JPMorgan Chase board backing of CEO Jamie Dimon through some tough times during the global financial crisis and more recently through the 2012 "London Whale" that cost the firm $6 billion in trading losses. Dimon's stand-up, totally transparent handling of the situation served him well. Added to these issues is the heat that was applied by investors because of Dimon's titles as chairman, president, and CEO as well as his compensation. With all that said, the board stuck with Jamie—and the stock has more than doubled since the "whale" beached itself.

The flipside of that coin is examples of boards moving to dismiss CEOs quickly and quietly when called for. Two examples are United Technologies in 2014 and United Airlines in 2015, each dismissing their CEOs for failed leadership and unacceptable conduct. Well done!

The Emergency Brake

I believe that government is too large, costs too much, spends too much, and has too much regulatory power in our lives.

—*Tim Walberg, Republican US Representative, Michigan*

If oversight is the brakes on the car, legal, regulatory, and audit (internal and external) are the emergency brake. Some, including Tim Walberg, regard these (particularly legal and regulatory) as necessary evils. From my experiences at Citibank and American Express, many line managers feel the same way about audit. My own experience, as both a player and a student/teacher of the realities of the business world, is different. I would argue that all these elements of the emergency brake on the business world have a long-term salubrious effect. One need only look to the global financial crisis of 2007/2008 where inadequate regulation played an important role.

When I think back to my CFO role at both the division and group level, I clearly recall my watchdog responsibilities to ensure that line managers (those actually running the businesses in the division or group) did not push our adherence to generally accepted accounting principles (GAAP) over the edge. They were constantly and aggressively on the lookout for ways to interpret GAAP in ways that would favor business results. I will get into more detail on that in the discussion of Enron (in the next chapter), but it is true in most businesses.

I have sat on the other side of the table when my treasury unit in the credit card group began the development of credit card securitization in 1989. With the help of First Boston (this was prior to the merger forming Credit Suisse First Boston), we essentially created the market for credit card securitization going from zero to more than $20 billion in credit card receivables securitized in just under eighteen months. Securitization was—and is—more expensive than non-securitization financing techniques due to higher structuring costs and an interest rate premium the market demands. That is because, while these structured financings were AAA rated, they are what is called *story paper* (in the selling process of the security, one must tell a more complicated story about them than in selling unstructured paper like general obligation debentures issued by Microsoft or Johnson & Johnson for example).

We were anxious to create this market and happy to pay this premium because securitized credit card receivables were counted as asset sales for accounting purposes and therefore were taken off the balance sheet. That meant, and continues to mean, that no capital is required to support the receivables. To make things even more complicated, this asset "sale" was—and is—treated as debt for tax purposes. It also behaved exactly like debt for our purposes.

In a manner of speaking, it walked like a duck (we continued to service the receivables, maintained the customer relationship, and had a strong economic interest in their performance) and talked like a duck (treated as debt for tax purposes), but GAAP and bank regulators allowed us to call it a chicken (treated as an asset sale and thus receivables came off the balance sheet and required no capital to support them). This was happening during the commercial real estate and savings-and-loan crisis of the early nineties when most banks, including Citibank, were short on capital. Taking $20 billion off the balance sheet and reducing Citibank's capital requirement by $1 to $2 billion was a big deal.

Making all these machinations work took a ton of documentation (a typical deal's legal paperwork was literally a book about four inches thick) and many tough discussions with our external auditors (then Peat Marwick and now KPMG). It seemed like my team, together with

First Boston, was regularly inventing new versions of this structure to give us more funding flexibility. Each kept pushing the edge of the GAAP envelope. With each new structure, we had to have another tough conversation with Peat Marwick to get their sign-off.

Where you stand in life depends on where you sit. On the one hand, I had to play cop, enforcing the law, and on the other, I was in the courtroom, arguing to stretch the law to meet corporate goals. All that being said, rules and regulations are necessary to keep the foxes at bay lest they take over the henhouse.

Oversight as Doing the Right Thing

Integrity has no need of rules.

—*Albert Camus*

In decisions that involve questions of integrity, I think there are a few rules of thumb that serve one well. These are tests you can subject your decisions too. Pick the one that resonates best with you. It will serve you well.

The first is the mirror test. How will you feel looking at yourself in the mirror daily if you take the action in question? The second I call the *New York Times* test. How would feel if your decision were to appear on the front page of tomorrow's edition of the *New York Times*? The third is the family test. How would you feel explaining your considered action to your mom, your spouse, or your kids? Note each of these tests involve how you would *feel*. The last is the fact that, in almost all situations involving integrity, the toughest path to walk is the one that is the right thing to do.

The Bottom Line

It ain't over till it's over.

—*Yogi Berra*

So, are you *fit* for decision-making? Are you a servant leader? Are you also a disciplined, buttoned-up manager? Do you have healthy oversight at your disposal? That's what you need, but it's also a very difficult combination to pull off. It is likely that you are weak in at least one of the three areas. Most of us are in any particular situation. Hopefully, reading this chapter will make you aware of your weaknesses and thus give you the opportunity to bolster them before making that important next decision. If you focus on the process and get the pieces right, your batting average will definitely improve. It's all a matter of checks and balances.

CHAPTER 6
ENRON: A CASE STUDY IN FAILED DECISION-MAKING

Enron and 9/11 marked the end of an era of individual freedom and the beginning of personal responsibility.

—*Jeffrey R. Immelt, CEO of General Electric (retired)*

The Enron story had been told in the news as it unfolded, several books were written about it, and a feature film was produced (*The Smartest Guys in the Room*). I will not try to recount this saga again, but I will extract from various sources, as necessary, to help the reader understand the lessons to be learned from the failure in the context of the Cube. My objective is to give the reader Proust's "new eyes," as mentioned in the preface, to view this saga and understand how the concepts of this book apply to this case study.

I don't purport that my explanations are complete, and other factors might not have been at play, but the factors I describe were major drivers of the failures. Therefore, the following descriptions are both distilled and selective.

Enteron—The Beginning

It's a little-known fact that, when InterNorth acquired Houston Natural Gas, the new company was first named Enteron. The name was the result of $100,000 in focus groups and consulting. When it was discovered that enteron is a medical term, usually with specific reference to the small intestine, the name was shortened to Enron. That was an inauspicious, though perhaps appropriate, beginning for sure.

Although InterNorth, headquartered in Omaha, Nebraska, acquired Houston Natural Gas (it had about three times the revenue of Houston Natural Gas), it was not long after the companies combined that Ken Lay, CEO of Houston Natural Gas, became CEO of Enron. The CEO of InterNorth was fired in the process. Masterfully done, Ken!

Shortly thereafter, he again masterfully engineered a move of the headquarters to Houston. That set the company on a path for an important cultural change from the Midwestern, Christian, conservative, pocket protector-wearing engineers of Omaha to the slick, wheeler-dealers of Houston. Houston was/is a city built on a swamp. It was a place where a man with a wildcatting spirit could transform himself virtually overnight; a like-minded company could remake itself, too.

Lay's press at the time indicated that he already had an impressive reputation. Barbara Cates Garnick, a natural gas expert at Cambridge Energy Research Associates regularly referred to Lay as one the most innovative men in the whole industry, Garnick was clearly on the right track. That capacity for innovation carried over to Lay's leadership. He created within Enron a purpose, context, and capacity for world-class innovation. "Ask why" was the company mantra. This will be clear at various intervals in the Enron story.

In some respects, Lay was a kind of Elon Musk in terms of innovation, but he had a fatal flaw that was not part of Musk's makeup. That was Lay's fixation on short-term earnings and Enron's day-to-day stock price movement (stock tickers were everywhere you went in Enron-Houston). Musk is, of course, all about the long term like Jeff Bezos and Mark Zuckerberg. In spite of that fatal flaw, under Lay's watch, Enron innovated tremendously. That's part of the reason why Wall Street turned a blind eye for so long regarding Enron's earnings' "black box."

I would not even accuse Lay as lacking a moral compass. That one lays squarely on the doorstep of CFO Andy Fastow and COO Skilling who will be discussed later in this chapter. Having thus given the devil his due regarding innovation, it's important to point out that Lay was also masterful at boardroom politics. Over several years after the merger of InterNorth and Houston Natural Gas, he engineered a shift in directors to a group handpicked by him and thus beholden to him.

The $2.3 billion transaction was announced May 3, 1985:

> The combination would create a giant energy corporation with the nation's second-largest natural-gas pipeline system, stretching from Canada to the Texas Panhandle and from California to Florida.

On December 3, 2001, one day after filing for bankruptcy, the press announced:

> Enron, which became one of the world's dominant energy companies by reshaping the way natural gas and electricity are bought and sold, filed the largest corporate bankruptcy in American history yesterday.

In comparing the two press releases, one of the things that stands out most is the change in the description of the company's business from "the nation's second-largest natural-gas pipeline system" to "reshaping the way natural gas and electricity are bought and sold." That transformation and how it unfolded was at the heart of the failure of Enron. So was deregulation—something that Ken Lay believed in passionately. Much of the Enron story is built around taking advantage of deregulation both strategically and tactically (opportunistically).

While many have argued that fraud drove the demise of the company, I will put forth the case that years of flawed business decision-making drove the failure. The fraud merely masked the flawed decision-making and prolonged the life of a dead man walking. This is also largely in line with the theme posited by Bethany McLean and Peter Elkind in their highly authoritative *The Smartest Guys in the Room: The Amazing Rise and Scandalous Fall of Enron*. I will draw from their work extensively and frame their treatise within the context of the Cube from chapter 1.

At its peak in August 2000, Enron's market capitalization (number of shares outstanding times share price, which essentially is the value the market is putting on the company) reached $60 billion. This was "seventy times earnings and six times book value, an indication of the stock market's high expectations about its future prospects." A company of that size does not declare bankruptcy a little over one year later from a few fraudulent transactions that resulted in tens of millions of dollars being misappropriated from the company's coffers (the capers of CFO Fastow and his minion Michael Kopper). As stated above, Enron's collapse occurred after more than a decade of poor decision-making, plain and simple.

To demonstrate my point, let's look at the numbers (based on Enron's Securities and Exchange Commission 10-K filing). This is the annual filing of financial results required by the SEC of all companies whose ownership is in the hands of the public. Enron's balance sheet showed total capitalization (debt plus equity) of $25.017 billion of which $11.470 billion was shareholders' equity (ownership interests), the balance being debt. Enron's off-balance-sheet debt brought estimated total liabilities to $67 billion. That, by the way, is a whopping $42 billion in off-balance transactions. There will be more on that later. In liquidation, shareholders got nothing, and debt holders got less than eighteen cents on the dollar. That says $67 billion in assets (on and off-balance sheet) shrunk to less than $12 billion. Clearly some of that was fire-sale pricing in the wake of forced asset liquidation, but most of it was the result of more than a decade of flawed decision-making hidden in those off-balance sheet transactions. In this Enron story, I will pursue those failed decisions.

The Beginning of the End

Suddenly the fingers of a human hand appeared and wrote on the plaster of the wall.

—*Daniel 5:5 KJV*

In many respects, the handwriting was on the wall for Enron in its earliest years. As mentioned above, Enron was essentially a natural gas pipeline company. However, it had an operation in Valhalla, New York, that traded oil futures. These are contracts that commit one party to supply a certain type of crude oil (there are various) to the "counterparty" at a prescribed date for a committed price. Folks use these contracts in the oil business to hedge (lock in the price today) for their oil needs (either to buy or to sell) in the future. Since the price is locked in, the forward market reduces or eliminates the risk associated with price fluctuation. These contracts were, and are today, also used by speculators who neither have any oil nor any need for it, but who want to bet on the future price of oil.

The Enron-Valhalla trading room, under the control of Louis Borget, delivered impressive profits to Enron head office every quarter like clockwork. That should have been the first warning that something was not right because proprietary trading (non-client-based trading for one's own account) has more volatility than that.

CEO Ken Lay purportedly loved it. What CEO wouldn't? However, he apparently had little sense of the risk being taken by the operation to generate those profits—until a routine audit uncovered a massive trading position that Borget had. He was betting that the price of oil would fall. When it didn't fall, Borget, convinced he was right, kept "doubling down" on his position rather than closing out the position and taking a loss. As McLean and Elkind put it, "The oil traders had come within a whisker of bankrupting the company."

The position was indeed massive.

> Enron was short over 84 million barrels. The position was so huge it amounted to roughly three months' output of the gigantic North Sea oil field off the coast of England. If Enron were forced to cover its position, it would have been on the hook for well over $1 billion.

The position was absurd for a company of Enron's size. Trading limits had been egregiously violated. "And, of course, given how strapped the company was for cash, there was simply no way it could cover its trading losses without filing for bankruptcy."

Lay sent senior executive Mike Muckleroy, an experienced commodities trader and a no-nonsense guy, to handle the situation. Muckleroy took command of the trading room (locking out Borget) and through a series of clever moves and some luck (prices actually declined somewhat), he masterfully wound down the position without the market becoming aware of it. As it was, the damage amounted to around $140 million—$85 million after taxes.

In terms of flawed decision-making and the Cube, it's pretty clearly that Borget acted irrationally, with action-oriented biases of overconfidence and overoptimism. As for Lay, we get our first glimpse of his position in the Cube through his irrationality in terms of misaligned goals/short-termism, a topic already discussed in chapter 2. This bias manifested itself in Lay's press for short-term earnings that naturally came at the cost of the long-term health of the firm.

Lay carried this issue over to create a flaw in his leadership in that he fostered the development of a culture that shared this same misaligned goal. That short-term focus in a business where most of the key decisions had long-range performance impact proved lethal. In Wall Street parlance, it's akin to "pump and dump."

CFO Andy Fastow characterized Enron's misaligned goals: "We were more concerned with creating earnings and not focused on long-term economic value. Had we been a private company, it may have been different." Frankly, I don't believe that. I think that short-termism was a disease that plagued Lay, Fastow, and most of Enron.

The Come-to-Jesus Meeting

The Lord is coming with fire, and his chariots are like a whirlwind; he will bring down his anger with fury, and his rebuke with flames of fire.

—*Isaiah 66:15*

Mike Seidl was a longtime friend of Lay's and served as president and COO through the Valhalla fiasco and beyond. However, Seidl suffered from many of the same weaknesses that plagued Lay. Both struggled to say no, and neither was worth a damn at confrontation. In other words, in terms of the Cube, they made a very poor CEO/COO combination (see chapter 5). There was zero management capacity between the two of them. In terms of the Cube, Enron was clearly over-led and undermanaged, which is a prescription for chaos. Valhalla was just one indication of that.

Along comes Rich Kinder. An attorney by education, Kinder was general counsel until Lay named him chief of staff. At that time, Lay had surrounded himself with a bunch of cronies, each with "ill-defined jobs and a line straight to the man who hired them. Morale was terrible. Backbiting had become part of the Enron culture. Power plays were a daily occurrence... All the politicking had practically paralyzed the company."

Kinder called an all-hands, come-to-Jesus meeting that changed the landscape. He made it clear to all present (including Lay) that there were "alligators in the swamp" that needed to be killed—and he was just the guy to do it. That was a turning point. Kinder was made president and COO in 1990, but he was de facto the man in charge after that 1988 meeting.

I would argue the Lay/Kinder combination was a healthier leader-manager duo than Enron had experienced since its formation, but Kinder could not shore up Lay's weaknesses as a leader. These were pointed out earlier in terms of the Cube as a misalignment of goals due to a myopic focus on short-term earnings.

Kinder was not a perfect manager. There were a number of terrible business decisions made on his watch (J-Bloc in the UK and Dabhol in India to name just two). Nonetheless, Kinder was demanding and brought sorely needed discipline to the C-suite. He was a manager, personified. He kept the trains running on time. When he left, that sorely needed skill set went with him and was not replaced. More on that later in this chapter.

Unbridled Genius

There is no great genius without some touch of madness.

—Aristotle

In 1987, Jeff Skilling, one of the youngest partners in McKinsey's history, came on the Enron scene. A Harvard "Baker Scholar" (top 5 percent of his class), Skilling was clearly one smart dude. In some respects, Skilling's arrival was just in time because Lay's Valhalla money machine had just died. He desperately needed a new big idea.

Skilling caught both Lay and Kinder's eye early on in his consulting work on the development of a "forward" market for natural gas (like the one for oil described in the Valhalla caper). Skilling called his idea the "Gas Bank." It would mirror a bank, but, rather than intermediate savers and borrowers as a traditional bank does, Skilling's plan called for Enron's Gas Bank to intermediate the "forward" transactions between buyers and sellers of natural gas. It was a brilliant idea.

Buyers were largely electric utilities. They abhorred the uncertainty of natural gas price volatility. It created earnings instability, an anathema, particularly in this industry, where stable, highly predictable earnings were the rule and not the exception. Being able to buy a natural gas forward contract and lock in the future needs at a price determined today was extremely attractive. They were clearly willing to pay a premium for this security.

Lay/Kinder enticed Skilling to join Enron in 1990 to supercharge the building of Lay's brainchild. Part of what attracted Skilling was the lucrative compensation scheme that tied his bonus compensation to the profits of the business he was going to run.

Skilling took his idea a step further.

Rather than be bound by the physical flow of the pipeline, Enron would become a stock market for natural gas. It was a magical new idea. Transform energy into financial instruments that could be traded like stocks or bonds.

Skilling said, "In 1992, we had become the largest buyer and seller of natural gas in North America."

This was a clear case of irrationality/misaligned goals/short-termism, yet everyone thought it was fine—including Arthur Anderson, Enron's outside auditor.

The Road to Perdition

The man who promises everything is sure to fulfill nothing, and everyone who promises too much is in danger of using evil means in order to carry out his promises, and is already on the road to perdition.

—Carl Jung

To fulfill the earnings' promise of the Gas Bank, Skilling insisted on *mark-to-market* accounting rather than traditional *historical cost accounting*. A full explanation of mark- to-market accounting is complicated, but it essentially consists of three features. The first is you get to recognize the potential future profits of a transaction on day one rather than spreading them over the transaction's life, irrespective of the timing of cash flows.

Obviously, this accelerates income recognition. That's great in the short term—today—but what about tomorrow? You have to do another transaction, and if you want to grow, you need to do two transactions, and so on. If you don't, you have no revenue on day two and/or no growth. From a business manager's standpoint (Skilling), this accounting is great in the early stages because growth is fast and malleable (see below). The mouse just must keep pedaling faster and faster.

The second is assets and associated liabilities must be "marked to market" at regular intervals with resulting gains and losses passed through the income statement. In the case of long-term (often ten or twenty years) natural gas contracts, there was no "market." So, Enron used models to estimate natural gas values into the distant future. Chapter 4 of this book covered the vagaries of models and the first three items in their construction are assumptions (the fourth is the technical construct of the model). In reality, Enron was not marking to market, they were "marking-to-model," which is a big difference.

But more important than their frailty to Enron was their malleability. Models are fraught with assumptions (as mentioned above) that could easily be tweaked in any given quarter to help hit earnings targets, either stretching to cover shortfalls or tightening to create cushion for future periods. Skilling did a spoof, playing himself in the skit, that described a "new, new method of accounting." He called it "hypothetical future value." To the skeptic, this said that Skilling's Gas Bank profits were whatever he wanted them to be.

The third feature of mark-to-market accounting is it facilitated the execution of Skilling's big idea. The market for natural gas was no longer bound to the physical delivery of the product. Enron proceeded to create a commodity market for natural gas that enabled it to be bought or sold like stocks or bonds—or perhaps more closely akin to oil and Louis Borget's operation in Valhalla.

For Skilling, who was building a new business, the first two conditions were ideal. This accounting treatment greatly facilitated his ability to grow the Gas Bank quickly and had strong earning predictability. These are two of the most important characteristics of a high-value business. And the ability to create futures contracts as a type of security that could be traded was more than the icing on the cake. It was a much bigger cake. Skilling was clearly a guy with big ideas, and this one was a winner.

However, mark-to-market accounting provides insight into how Skilling ran amuck of the Cube with misaligned goals/short-termism. Also, since he had a direct financial interest in the short-term profits of his division by way of his bonus scheme he suffered the bias of misaligned incentives. Together, these caused him to act in a manner that proved detrimental to the long-term health of the business and the company. Later, when he became president and chief operating officer, he and Lay as CEO were a lethal combination to the long-term health of Enron since they shared these two biases. In combination, the two were like nitro and glycerin coming together to make nitroglycerin.

Mark the Shark, aka the Empress of Energy[18]

Rebecca Mark named "one of the luckiest people in Houston."

—Fortune

Rebecca Mark (now Rebecca Mark-Jusbasche) was yet another of the "best and the brightest." Mark graduated from Harvard Business School with an MBA while working part-time for Enron. She did it the hard way, with her two young twins in tow, as a single parent. Later in her career, she became head of Enron Development, which subsequently became Enron International.

When she stepped off Enron jets in remote spots in third world countries, she was welcomed like a celebrity and surrounded by throngs of reporters. Mark was a high-profile woman in a male industry at the time when building power plants and pipelines across the globe was thought to be one of the most glamorous, profitable businesses ever, a little like the Internet in the late 1990s.

---

18. bid.

Mark was much more than smart. She was a highly competent manager and a first-class marketer and negotiator. Also, the one word that comes up in most every description of her is *glamorous*, an attribute she cultivated and apparently used to her advantage in business. To her credit, she was named to Fortune's "50 Most Powerful Women" in American business in both 1998 and 1999.

Here is a summary of her philosophy and mission in her business career:

We are brought together with a certain amount of missionary zeal which I think you have to have in this business. It demands so much of you all the time that you have to believe in what you're doing. I think for us that missionary zeal has three parts—first, that these projects are good for the country. They get the economy moving by bringing in power and they bring in investment. Second, these plants are environmentally safe and without equal when you consider the options of coal or nuclear power. Third, we are bringing a market mentality and spreading the privatization gospel in countries that desperately need this kind of thinking.

The passion is laudable, and I don't mean that dismissively. I truly admire it. It's required in both sound leadership and management and, indeed, in work in general to foster engagement. But there are a few yellow lights here. I will refer back to the above quote as we proceed through the saga of Mark's "big enchilada" as Skilling liked to call Enron's big bets.

In the late eighties and early nineties, Mark had many successes under her belt building power-generation facilities and gas pipelines in less developed countries. Then she went after the big one in India: the Dabhol Power Station. The total project was to produce 2,440 megawatts and was to be built in two phases. Phase 1 was 740 megawatts fueled by naphtha. Phase II was 1,700 mega-watts fueled by liquefied natural gas (LNG), Enron's energy source of choice. Note this was more than ten times the original requirement advertised by the Indian government that initiated discussions with Enron.

Enron had entered into a partnership with the Qatari government for LNG, and fuel supplies for Dabhol would come from this source. The construction of the Dabhol plant would be accompanied by the development of a modern port facility capable of unloading large tankers for equipment and LNG, and the development of a regasification facility to vaporize the LNG prior to its being used in the gas turbines.

The total price tag was over $3 billion. In the end, Enron lost over $1 billion on the project.

In many respects, this was Mark trying to replicate the success of Enron's Teesside project in the UK, but in India. Going back to the Cube, this was pattern recognition bias/false analogy—in spades. For starters, India is a long way from the UK, literally and figuratively.

Going back to the statement of Mark's "mission and philosophy" described in the earlier quote, the first yellow light is the implication of her first point. More power, more investment. So, bigger is better, right? Yes, better for Mark and Enron. For Mark, the bigger the project, the bigger the bonus, the bigger her job became, and the greater chance she had to reach the pinnacle of power at Enron. Her ambition was boundless. This was a case of misaligned incentives, for sure. For Enron, it had to be big to move the earnings needle and make a splash in the press. Then, it would be another gold star. It was a clear case of short-termism.

For India, bigger was not better. In 2017, some twenty-five years later, Dabhol is still underutilized and sitting on a mountain of debt ($1.6 billion), in spite of all the write-offs (Enron alone wrote off $1 billion) and government subsidies it has enjoyed over the years. This was a very, very bad deal for India all around. Why did it do it? My guess is that, at the time, the new government was looking for a hallmark foreign direct investment (FDI) that would capture the world's attention and deliver a message that FDI was now welcomed in India. The country has waxed and waned on FDI both before and since that time. In terms of the Cube, India suffered from misaligned goals/ short-termism.

The second point she mentions is that, yes, LNG is far more environmentally friendly than coal. However, coal is abundantly available in India, while all LNG must be imported and is far costlier than coal. It begs the question, Could India afford cleaner air from a massive LNG-fired power plant? I think the answer came from a World Bank study that spoke out against the Dabhol project. Hired by the

Indian government, the World Bank "circulated a report concluding that the Dabhol plant would create years of excess baseload capacity and prove an expensive alternative to coal or other fuels." So, its economics were doomed from the start. In terms of the Cube, for Enron, this was a case of action-oriented bias/overoptimism in forecasting the need for power in Maharashtra State. The same was true for India. There were many action-oriented biases on this one.

The third yellow light was Mark's comment about privatization. India is still a mixed economy some twenty-five years later. I think it's arrogant for a multinational enterprise like Enron to attempt to influence the form of government of a country where it's a guest—except in the case of corruption or mitigation of violence. In other words, it's one thing for an American company like Enron to lobby for deregulation in its home country, which it did relentlessly, but it's another to behave this aggressively when you are a guest in a foreign country. I think this is beyond the action-oriented bias of overconfidence. It is hubris, plain and simple.

There were multiple biases at play in Dabhol, and some action-oriented ones have already been mentioned. One of the stability biases was the sunk-cost fallacy. Joe Sutton, Mark's head of Asian operations, said:

> The fact is that we've already invested $13.2 million with Bechtel and GE (General Electric) on this project, so we're very committed … If we didn't believe in this project and its importance to India we wouldn't be doing it.

An associate of mine was a senior executive of Dabhol from 2000 until 2002, right through Enron's final days and beyond. I'll call him Peter. He has the greatest respect to this day for what he saw as the professionalism, innovative spirit, and hardworking ethos that was an integral part of the Enron culture. That's a lot coming from Peter who is a cum laude graduate of both Yale and Harvard.

For sure, the Dabhol team accomplished some impressive things. In the midst of the 1997 Asian currency crisis, when credit markets were in turmoil, Dabhol managed to put together a major financing, a remarkable feat under the circumstances. Peter, who remains associated with the power-generation industry, has commented that he frequently runs into ex-Enron employees in his work. That's not surprising since they were after all the "smartest guys in the room," both figuratively and literally.

Notwithstanding the quality of its staff, Dabhol was ill-fated on many fronts. Phase 2 was to be fueled by natural gas, all of which was to be imported from Qatar. It was being fueled by natural gas because that's what Enron did—not coal, which is what India had. It was massive in part because Enron International's developers, Mark's team, were paid bonuses on the size of the deal they did and they were paid when the contracts were signed and the financing was put in place—well before the plant was operational.

> And the money they stood to make was stunning, amounting to some 9 percent of the project's total value. In other words, if the developers estimated the project would ultimately bring Enron $100 million, the developers took home $9 million. In a sense, they were paid on the basis of mark-to-market accounting—just like the traders in Skilling's group.

This motivated Mark and her developers to do big deals—fast—and move on to the next deal. The incentives weren't aligned with the long-term benefits of the shareholders. Again, we see misaligned goals and short-termism.

In terms of the Cube and complexity, Dabhol was both highly complicated (at its height, it employed fifteen thousand people) and highly complex. Mark was certainly on top of the former and was reasonably adept at the latter, but the complexity got the better of her and, for a time, she lost control of the project. The population of India turned against Dabhol and against Enron in general. The expedited bidding process was harshly criticized by the opposition political party that came into power in the middle of the project. They stopped Dabhol II and ended up in arbitration in London. Enron made some concessions (greater ownership of Dabhol to Maharashtra State Power Development Corporation and reduced charges for the electricity). Still, its energy was to be India's most expensive source of electricity by multiples of the next-highest provider.

Mark exited Enron in 2000 beautifully, selling her stock for a reported $82 million. "She was never accused of wrongdoing in the ensuing series of scandals and prosecutions." Mark now operates cattle ranches in Colorado and New Mexico.

Good for her, but that doesn't change the fact that she destroyed more than $1 billion in shareholder value with her decisions on Dabhol and another $1 billion with the Azurix caper that is briefly described in the next section. In terms of the Cube, her decisions were fraught with action-oriented biases, the stability sunk-cost bias, a pattern-recognition bias of a false analogy (Dabhol/Teeside), and managing the complicated but failing to lead the complex. Perhaps the government change with accompanying charges of misconduct in the midst of Dabhol might be considered a black swan (though a part of any emerging market investment should consider the possibility of a regime change and have contingency plans for coping). With Azurix, as you will see, it was a clear case of false analogies. So, she pretty much hit most all the key drivers of failed decision-making.

Fastow Creates a Fog of War

The fog of war is the uncertainty in situational awareness experienced by participants in military operations.[19]

In Skilling's constant battle to develop the next big idea, show strong growth in current earnings, and—perhaps most importantly—hide mistakes, he had a strong ally in his protégé. Andy Fastow was Enron's chief financial officer (CFO). Hiding mistakes was Fastow's specialty, and in so doing, he created a fog of war for the Wall Street analysts. He held all of the cards, knowing the reality of Enron's actual performance, and he created a fog hovering over their financial statements that was virtually impenetrable. Enron's earnings were regularly referred to as a "black box" by Wall Street analysts. Hindsight is twenty-twenty, but it is remarkable that they accepted Enron's performance as presented. Warren Buffett has sagely said never invest in something you don't understand, yet very smart people did—to the tune of a $70 billion market cap at its peak.

---

19. "Fog of War," Wikipedia.

Of course, this is not unique to Enron. Herd psychology creates asset bubbles all the time. I would suggest that the stock market's love affair with President Trump at the time of this writing (September 1, 2017) could very well prove to be one of those "black box" asset bubbles.

I had a one-on-one meeting with Fastow for half an hour before he addressed a group of American University students. He's a paid speaker on the subject of the impact of structured financing. An affable guy, perhaps a bit cocky, he talked quite freely about his role in engaging in a plethora of structured financings. His shtick is that all of his transactions were approved by attorneys, lawyers, senior management (read Lay/Skilling), and the board of directors:

> I did not embezzle, avoid taxes, or do any sort of insider trading. What I am guilty of is creating financial structures that made Enron look better to the public than it actually was. Accounting rules can be vague and we at Enron viewed that vagueness as an opportunity."

> I looked at that situation, Enron as an institution looked at that situation, and said, "When there's ambiguity, when there's complexity, when the rules don't exist, that's not a problem, that's an opportunity," Fastow said. "By using the law to your advantage. It didn't matter if it was ethical or unethical."[20]

The courts took issue with Fastow's opening remarks. He and his associate Michael Kopper took tens of millions in fees from highly questionable (conflict of interest) ownership positions in certain of Fastow's structured deals. His wife, Lea, served a year in prison for tax fraud related to misreporting income, but Fastow has his shtick, and he's sticking to it.

The business world today continues to do the same things that Enron did he maintains—and worse. "It makes me blush," says Fastow. Clearly that takes a lot.

Fastow's job was masking true operating results, and he did it brilliantly, but he was overcome with greed. He structured deals to

---

20."Post-Prison, Former Enron CFO Hits Speaking Circuit," Nushin Huq, *Bloomberg Law*, February 19, 2016.

earn big bonuses, and he did them with personal payments to himself and at least one associate: Michael J. Kopper.

In fact, Kopper was the first high-ranking Enron employee to be found guilty of lying and stealing some $16 million.[21] Kopper worked directly with and for Fastow in crafting the byzantine structures that took Enron's mistakes off their balance sheet and out of their income statements.

> It did not take long for Mr. Kopper, an eager Nick Carraway susceptible to the lure of Mr. Fastow's Gatsby, to join his mentor in Houston in 1994.[22]

And the rest, as they say, is history.

The Big Enchilada

Skilling used to publicly predict that EES would one day be bigger than all of the rest of Enron.[23]

Enron Energy Services (EES) was not just a step away—it was a giant leap away from anything Enron had ever done. There were no false analogies as in Dabhol with Teesside. EES was Enron's foray into delivering energy at the retail level to both homes and businesses. Its success was highly dependent on deregulation. In spite of—or perhaps because of—Skilling's heavy-handed muscling of congressmen, the lobbying efforts failed, even in their home state of Texas. That left only the business market, but that was plenty big enough. Enron went after it with hammer and tongs.

Curiously, EES was a Skilling brainchild that he first gave to Fastow to develop before Andy was made CFO. Fastow had been pining away for a business management position for some time because that was where the prestige and money was. It was not in staff positions. By Fastow's own account in my one-on-one with him, he could not figure out, for the life of him, how you could make it in the business. After nine months of failed effort, Skilling took him off of it. Fastow thought

21. Ibid.
22. Ibid.
23. *"The Smartest Guys in the Room: The Amazing Rise and Scandalous Fall of Enron,"* Bethany McLean and Peter Elkind, Penguin Press, 2003.

his career at Enron was over, but Skilling saw him as a creative genius for structured finance. Not long afterward, Fastow was made CFO at the remarkably young age of thirty-seven. I imagine nobody was more surprised than Fastow himself.

At Skilling's behest, Lou Pai led the charge at EES. Pai had led the trading room activities successfully, but he knew as much about satisfying business's energy needs as Mark did about water and Ken Rice did about broadband: nothing! There is more about Mark and water and Rice and broadband in the next section. Skilling specifically—and Enron overall—believed that if you could manage, you could manage anything. I, however, believe that experience counts. I refer you back to chapter 2 on irrationality and the section on bounded rationality. It explains how experience expands *computational intelligence* and permits rational intuitive decision-making. Without it, you are lost. Hence, my position on Citigroup's choice of Chuck Prince as CEO (covered in the last chapter).

EES's *core-value proposition* was managing (note that key word: managing) long-term contracts with businesses to supply their energy needs. Enron's compensation was linked to the savings it would deliver over time, often through the purchase of up-to-date equipment for their customers. Sometimes Enron even made an up-front payment to their customers for entering into the long-term contract. And the icing on the cake was that EES used mark-to-market accounting! Yikes!

In my one-on-one with Andy Fastow, he told me that he discovered one day that Pai had booked $150 million in mark-to-market earnings that apparently "even made me blush." There he goes with that blushing thing again.

On the face of it, Pai was not a bad choice for a person to run EES. He showed the leadership skills to successfully run the trading room with great success. However, to succeed at EES, he needed strong, Kinder-like management skills. Skilling was smart enough to recognize this and decided a CEO/COO combo would be best. So, Tom White, a retired general who had successfully managed the construction of Teesside, took the reins as Pai's number two. Even with this, EES was chaos.

Enron was great at negotiating contracts. That's complex. Enron was abominable at execution. It was awful at block-and-tackle management. The nuts-and-bolts stuff was unsexy and wasn't apt to get you much of a bonus. From reading *The Smartest Guys in the Room: The Amazing Rise and Scandalous Fall of Enron*, I got the sense that management skills were regarded with a certain amount of disdain at Enron, particularly after Kinder left. That was something the gas pipeline guys did—and they all punch clocks and wear pocket protectors, right? Maybe they even get paid by the hour.

What EES could do was win contracts though, as evidenced by the extract below.

> Tom White won EES the first contract for privatization of utility management at a US military base. Enron even claimed the blessing of the Roman Catholic Church: a seven-year energy deal with the Archdiocese of Chicago. In 1998, Enron announced, EES has signed contracts with a total "value" of $3.8 billion. By the end of 1999, the company had signed up so many new customers that the "total contract value," according to Enron, was a stunning $8.5 billion.

Indeed, Enron certainly could win business. On bigger deals, Lay himself would go out and do a dog and pony show. It was all hands on deck to make EES real. Enron even invented its own metric: total contract value (TCV). It sounded great, and if dot-coms could measure eyeballs, hits, and stickiness as a way to take everyone's eyes off profits, why couldn't Enron/EES do the same with TCV? Everybody was making stuff up in those halcyon days before the dot-com bubble burst.

In the first couple of years, the market was clearly unhappy with the EES venture as Skilling was breaking his pick in the retail market. Jefferies & Company energy analyst Larry Crowley was perhaps the most positive of Wall Street's analysts. "Crowley's own view was that EES could become 'a major home run.' But he acknowledged that investor concern over 'the size of the bet' resulted in Wall Street giving Enron 'zero value' for EES."

But Enron took steps to change that zero valuation as Fastow stepped in to work his magic. He found two buyers who were willing to make a minority investment in EES (7 percent) for $130 million. They were JEDI II (CalPERS) and the Ontario Teacher's Pension Plan, both purportedly smart money. The deal did three things:

> First, it helped offset the retail business's start-up costs. Second, Enron used the investment to establish a franchise value for all of EES, the reasoning being that if 7 percent of the business was worth $130 million, the entire effort was worth $1.9 billion— about $5.50 per Enron share … Here's the third thing the deal did: it allowed Enron to book a $61 million profit in 1997. That amounted to 58 percent of the company's net earnings for the year… keeping the earnings … from being even more dismal than they already were.

In spite of all that, Enron recognized that organic growth would be too slow, both for its own ambitions and to meet Wall Street's lofty expectations. Back to the Cube, irrationality/action-oriented bias/misaligned goals/short-termism was rearing its ugly head. So, it embarked on a *roll-up campaign* of acquisitions. This term is applied when a large competitor buys up a string of small competitors so it can dominate the industry.

Acquisitions have a history of failure (as previously discussed in chapter 1), but a roll-up strategy is far less risky as long as the execution is sound. And acquisitions have their advantages. They are fast because you buy a customer base and revenue stream. If you're good at it, you can drastically reduce or even eliminate the expense base (largely employees) of the acquired firm. The financial impact can be dramatically positive—and you can learn how to acquire and integrate the acquirees as you go since the cost of learning from failure and trial and error is small. All of this is possible if you pace yourself and do it right. Enron, pace itself and do it right? Not likely—and indeed it didn't.

EES was so disorganized that it was incapable of doing simple things like correctly billing its customers. Here's an excerpt from *The Smartest Guys in the Room* coming from a customer, Cal State administrator David De Mauro.

> "There were no situations," he says, "where the bills were either on time or correct. People either didn't get the bills or they got incorrect bills. We went all four years without receiving

timely or accurate bills … We probably went five or six months without paying Enron at all. I would guess our accounts payable was approaching $40 million or so."

No wonder EES was hemorrhaging cash. With making front-end payments to win contracts and the cost of acquisitions, money was flowing out like water out of a fire hose.

Unlike most of Enron's forays that were solid business ideas just ahead of their time or well-conceived ideas that were poorly executed, EES, to my knowledge, never caught on as a great business idea anywhere—at least not on the scale that Enron envisioned. Outsourcing systems development and management is a well-established business. I described my experience with it in the story about the One-Bank Partnership Team earlier in the book. Energy services was not a well-established business, and I believe that is true to this day.

Going back to the Cube, like most of Enron's failed decisions, EES was clearly a case of irrational action-oriented biases (both overconfidence and overoptimism) and misaligned goals (short-termism) that permeated virtually all Enron's fiascos. It was a case of a business where organizational fitness went awry since it was over-led and undermanaged—a lot like Enron itself.

For EES to have succeeded would have required tight, military-fashion management. Perhaps that was available in the pipeline business or in parts of Mark's world, but it was certainly not part of Pai's DNA—even with his number two in tow. The Teesside general was just not enough. EES was a major flop.

Let a hundred flowers blossom.

—Chairman Mao Zedong

Skilling's appetite to drive up the stock price was insatiable, and so was his pattern-recognition bias. He was extraordinarily successful with a model of commoditization and securitization of energy (natural gas and electricity), and he tried to apply it with a couple of different businesses where it just didn't work, namely water (a business called Azurix) and broadband.

Azurix, from the Cube, represented pattern-recognition bias (false analogy). It was a business to be built by acquisitions, a perilous road to take for any business, except for the classic roll-up strategy. In water, the acquisitions were huge and perilous. One of infamy for Enron was the Buenos Aires waterworks. Enron not only bid more than $300 million (ten times) more than its closest competitor, it ended up not buying a real business. It was buying more of a license to do business. There was a successful acquisition of sorts: Essex in the UK. It was more or less a success in that the profitability of the business was meager versus its purchase price, but at least it was profitable.

Skilling, wanting Mark out of his hair, convinced the board to spin off the water business, under the name of Azurix, into the public markets with Mark as CEO. The allure of being a CEO of a publicly held company was strong for Mark. She jumped at the chance only to see Azurix falter. Enron ended up buying back Azurix, and shortly thereafter, Mark made a graceful exit, selling all of her Enron stock for a cool $85 million as previously mentioned. "How a Fledgling Water Business Helped Sink Enron" was the headline for an article sent out by the Associated Press that portrayed the problems at Azurix as "act I in the wreckage of Enron." I estimate Azurix cost Enron about $1 billion in losses. That would then be a total of $2 billion that Mark cost Enron.

And then there was broadband. This one was, in terms of the Cube, Skilling's short-termism at its finest as well as pattern-recognition bias (false analogy). At its core, this business revolved around selling bandwidth as a commodity. Building the network was just a means to that end. The *false analogy* was that broadband was going to be fashioned like natural gas. Enron owned the pipeline and traded the commodity. The difference was that broadband bandwidth was not a commodity. That is to say that broadband bandwidth was differentiated. Bandwidth carrying the Super Bowl had a much different value than the bandwidth that delivers a movie to your hotel room. Nonetheless, here's how Skilling saw the numbers for broadband:

> According to Skilling's back-of-the-envelope calculation— "horseshoes and hand grenades," he liked to call it—Enron's market value would increase by $20 for every dollar the

company invested in a broadband venture. Thus, a $1 billion investment would add $20 billion in market capitalization. Whether the business would bring in cash or profits (and how long this might take)—those were different issues.

So, sure enough, when Enron's entry into broadband was announced, the stock price jumped over 30 percent in two days. In terms of the Cube, this was an example of Wall Street's irrationality—irrationality with an action-oriented bias of overoptimism. According to Skilling:

> "I've always believed there's no such thing as a free lunch," he later told associates, "but this looks like a free lunch."

The deal with Blockbuster collapsed, but "Enron managed to book $53 million in earnings in a deal that didn't make them a penny in profits." That takes us right back to the Cube and Enron's maniacal focus on short-term earnings. This is why Fastow was such a hero. He had the Midas touch—except he was turning dog poop into platinum!

I have to give the devil his due. The broadband deal with Blockbuster preceded movie streaming by more than ten years. That's the risk of backing an idea ahead of its time. To this day, bandwidth is still not traded—so that part was just a bad idea.

Organizational Fitness Gone Awry

Leadership, management, and oversight were all fatally flawed at Enron. In fairness, Lay and Skilling fostered some healthy aspects of the corporate culture as part of their leadership responsibilities. The famous "ask why" mentality was laudable and fostered an environment of creativity and innovation. Creativity and innovation were hallmarks of the Enron culture. One must give the devil his due there as well.

Enron was a classic example of what happens when a firm is over-led and undermanaged—it's chaos. Once Kinder left, management skills deteriorated fast. And why wouldn't they? Neither Lay or Skilling valued them. They were both big on ideas and not execution. Skilling and Lay had some strong leadership qualities, but both were fatally flawed as leaders. They shared the bias of misaligned goals or short-termism. Having said that, neither had a management bone in his body. "Vision without execution is hallucination." Lay and Skilling were hallucinating big-time for years.

In addition, risk-taking, another Enron trait, was out of control. And that was due to the fact that Enron's oversight of internal controls was extraordinarily weak. It did not have a control mentality, despite the protestations of Skilling and Lay to the contrary. The first level of defense was the risk assessment and control department (RAC), which was run by Rick Buy. RAC had the resources (a $30 million budget, access to a $600 million computer system, and 150 professionals.) to perform analytically robust analyses of proposed deals and had the ability to "tell management 'do not proceed.'" RAC was an integral part of the sales pitch to Wall Street analysts, and it was done in classic slick Enron fashion. Wall Street was dazzled, but the reality was different from the pitch. Surprise, surprise!

Amongst the company's deal makers, RAC was a joke. They didn't take RAC seriously and for good reason:

> "The mentality was to do whatever they can to go over, under, and right through us; that was the objective," says one RAC veteran.

Buy's own admissions indicate that he viewed RAC as part of the deal-doing process—and not as oversight or as the brakes on a car. Where was the oversight? Where were the checks and balances? I would suggest there were none. The board was a rubber stamp.

Fastow, in his own words during the presentation he made, said he had an Excel spreadsheet with the numbers of the off-balance-sheet special purpose entities that showed how Enron's credit rating went from a A- to the reality of a CCC- (a notch just above junk bonds) if all the SPEs were brought back on the balance sheet. One of the board members, by Fastow's personal account, said, "Fastow, you're a fucking genius!" I could tell by the way he said it that he was still proud of that moment.

Three Strikes—and You're Out!

While Enron ran afoul of almost every concept leading to failed decision-making embodied in the Cube, undoubtedly the big three were action-oriented biases (overconfidence and overoptimism), misaligned goals (short-termism), pattern-recognition biases (false analogies), and not being able to manage the *complicated* in Enron Energy Services. Enron did much better with the complex (profiting in fast-moving markets it often created), though Mark ran amuck of the complex with Dabhol in India.

And then came uncertainty in the form of the giant black swan that was the dot-com bubble bursting in 2001. That was pretty much game time for Enron. As its stock price collapsed below $30/share, most of Fastow's magical deals, collateralized by Enron stock, started to reverse and come back on Enron's balance sheet with their associated losses. It was a bloodbath for the company in the third and fourth quarters of 2001. And so, on December 2, 2001, Enron threw in the towel.

That's a Wrap!

It is surely not a bum rap. Enron's Icarus-like descent was followed by a merciless pursuit by the Department of Justice of the company's miscreants. People did serous jail time for their roles in Enron, and well they should have. There was illegal activity in numerous areas. The Department of Justice had a field day getting people to turn state's evidence with Skilling and Lay as specific targets.

Most, though not all, of this illegal activity was built around masking Enron's true operating results from security analysts and investors— Wall Street. The Street determines the marginal *cost of capital* of a firm. In other words, the Street determines what it costs the firm, in terms of rate of return demanded by investors, at the margin, to raise its next dollar of capital. That cost of capital is based on the Street's perceived risk/reward balance for the firm. In this respect, the Street is an important source of oversight for publicly traded companies. If the firm is delivering a poor risk/reward tradeoff, the market will raise its cost of capital (drive the price of its stock down and reduce its credit rating, thus raising the interest rate on its borrowings).

Fastow's fog and mark-to-market (read: mark-to-model) accounting prevented the Street from doing its job. One could argue greater skepticism should have been in order and would have dampened market over-exuberance, but this occurred at the apex of the dot-com bubble. The fundamentals of valuation had gone out the window, generally speaking. The crisp, clear, and dispassionate analysis required to appropriately assess the value of securities fell by the wayside. If Enron had been transparent in its reporting, it would not have been able to raise the capital it did to fund ill-fated ventures like Dabhol, broadband, water, and retail-energy services to name a few of the biggest.

I reviewed Enron's 2000 annual report as well as its 10K for 2000 as previously mentioned. While I'm not an accountant, I was a senior credit officer in my later years at Citibank. In that position, I got to analyze myriad financial statements and accompanying footnotes. I never saw anything remotely close to Enron's spiderweb of transactions. To say the reporting was opaque doesn't do it justice. The balance sheet was a black hole, and the income statement was a black box.

Enron's stock peaked at $90/share (market cap of $70 billion) in August 2000, just sixteen months before it reached its nadir and filed for bankruptcy. The 2000 annual report, in hindsight, reads like a fairy tale—a Grimm's fairy tale.

When the dot-com bubble burst in 2001, Enron's stock fell precipitously below $30 a share in the third quarter. This caused various of Fastow's structures (the ones collateralized with Enron stock) to collapse. The assets came back on Enron's balance sheet, and their related losses hit Enron's income statement. Enron's debt was downgraded, and cash-collateral clauses were triggered on many of its trades. It was a classic run on the bank. Skilling's dream of hitching Enron's stock to the dot-com boom turned into a nightmare. The rest, as they say, is history.

It's ironic that Enron appeared as number 5 on the 2002 Fortune 500 list of the largest companies some six months after it declared bankruptcy. That was because the rules for determining a company's position on the list are based on the first nine months of the company's reported earnings of the prior year. Enron declared bankruptcy on December 2, 2001, which was well after the close of the third quarter. So, Enron flaunted the spirit of the rules to achieve its bigger-than-life objective one final time.

CHAPTER 7
THE END

Work expands so as to fill the time available for its completion.
—Parkinson's law

Normally, this would be the epilogue, but I believe that all things come in odd numbers and not even ones. And so, when this book ended up with six chapters, the epilogue became chapter 7. Call me superstitious, but I chalk it up to poetic license. Whatever! Here it is.

Finally! Indeed, writing a book is not a sprint; it's a marathon. For me, it was almost five years in the making. The three most profound things I learned from the experience are: first, like data, if you torture words long enough, they will confess to anything; second, it's just as hard to write a bad book as it is to write a good book; third, you don't know which you are writing until the readers tell you! I anxiously await your verdict.

These past five years have been a tortuous journey. In some respects, I wouldn't trade it for the world, but in other respects, I wouldn't wish it on my worst enemy. As just one example of the torture, it took me two and a half years to write chapter five, and I'm still not happy with it.

But, no matter, the deed is done. You be the judge.

ABOUT THE AUTHOR

Professor Sicina has thirty years of experience in senior executive positions at Citibank, American Express, and various entrepreneurial endeavors. He worked for fourteen years in Latin America for Citibank, where he served as country manager of Colombia and division chief financial officer (CFO). He became CFO of Citibank's entire International Consumer Group and, later, of Citibank's US credit card business. Professor Sicina subsequently joined American Express and went on to become president of American Express Bank Ltd. and a member of its board of directors. Subsequently, he was named president of the Latin American division for the corporation. Professor Sicina has since worked in executive positions of several entrepreneurial endeavors. As part of his coursework, he leads student teams that help entrepreneurs in post-conflict regions create business plans. He also is a member of the international advisory board of Partners of the Americas.

www.ingramcontent.com/pod-product-compliance
Lightning Source LLC
Chambersburg PA
CBHW051308120626